Putin and His Neighbors

Putin and His Neighbors

Russia's Policies Toward Eurasia

Dina R. Spechler and Martin C. Spechler

LEXINGTON BOOKS
Lanham • Boulder • New York • London

Published by Lexington Books
An imprint of The Rowman & Littlefield Publishing Group, Inc.
4501 Forbes Boulevard, Suite 200, Lanham, Maryland 20706
www.rowman.com

Unit A, Whitacre Mews, 26-34 Stannary Street, London SE11 4AB

British Library Cataloguing in Publication Information Available

Library of Congress Control Number: 2019914200

ISBN 978-1-4985-8871-3 (cloth)
ISBN 978-1-4985-8873-7 (pbk)
ISBN 978-1-4985-8872-0 (electronic)

In memory of our parents
Sidney and Dorothy Spechler
Sydney and Beatrice Rome
with gratitude for their unwavering love and support.

Russia and Its Neighbors. Created by Jacob Schumacher.

Contents

Introduction

Our book analyzes the policies of the Russian Federation toward the countries that surround it. We think these policies have been central to both the successes and the weaknesses of President Vladimir Putin's overall foreign policy. In Chapter 1 we outline what appear to be Putin's chief foreign policy objectives and the means Russia has employed to achieve those objectives since he assumed the presidency in 2000. Chapter 2 identifies the sources of Russia's material weaknesses, clearly in evidence since 2014, which have had a substantial impact on the country's external behavior. Moscow has sought to advance Russian interests in its entire neighborhood by means of the regional institutions we discuss in Chapter 3. We then turn in Chapter 4 to the first group of Russia's neighbors, the five ex-Soviet countries to its immediate south. In this region Russia has attempted to court authoritarian leaders and to engage their efforts against terrorism and drug trafficking by providing material support. Next, in Chapter 5, we take up those five ex-Soviet states whose loyalty Russia has sought to assure by providing armed support or by engaging in military intervention and occupation. Chapter 6 deals with Russia's responses, with grudging cooperation from Belarus, to the states on its northwest border which have joined or associated with NATO in recent years. Chapter 7 focuses on the increasing power of China and Moscow's attempt to establish mutually beneficial cooperation with the People's Republic, both in Russia's neighborhood and worldwide. Our conclusion (Chapter 8) summarizes Putin's moderately successful foreign policy towards Russia's neighbors and speculates on possible future developments when Putin's influence no longer dominates the scene.

We argue that Putin's approach to his neighbors reflects his determination to restore Russia's great power status. However, he has had to consider the available ways and means to do this. What part of tax revenue, resources, or imports from abroad must be devoted to domestic consumption, essential to preserve the regime's power? How much must be saved, and how much can be devoted to arms? He has also had to consider the strengths and vulnerabilities of each of the neighboring countries he has sought to deal with. To estimate these, in Chapters 3-6 we outline briefly the geographic, demographic, economic, and military defense situations of these states. How have the leaders in these countries responded to Russian initiatives and policies? Some have been friendly, some isolationist, others eager to limit Russia's influence, but none have been indifferent to what Russia does. Their age, background, and political standing with their own elites and politically engaged publics have been important, as they have been for Putin himself.

According to our liberal perspective, the political outlooks and objectives of individual leaders and their need to satisfy the demands of influential elites and other domestic constituents play crucial roles in foreign policy decisions. This is true even in authoritarian states. It is even more the case in Putin's Russia, a "mixed regime" which combines tremendous power in the hands of a single leader with democratic institutions such as an elected president and national legislature. Putin clearly dominates foreign policy decision-making, but he is highly sensitive to the interests and opinions of elites whose support he needs and to the opinions of the voting public. Thus our study attaches considerable weight to Putin's views and the ideas and assumptions on which they are based, but it likewise highlights the role of elites and publics in shaping his calculations. At the same time, we pay considerable attention to the material bases of power in Russia's relations with its neighbors. In short, we adopt a multi-factor approach to understanding foreign policy that takes into account both domestic factors and states' relative economic and military power.

Since the collapse of the Soviet Union in 1991, the state over which Moscow presides has suffered a considerable decline in demographic, economic and military strength. But with its vast resources, the role it has inherited in the United Nations and the world's largest nuclear arsenal, Russia still plays an extremely important role on the world stage and is likely to do so for the foreseeable future. It is therefore essential to understand its ambitions and the strategies, instruments and techniques it employs in an effort to realize those ambitions. This book aims to contribute to such an understanding.

Chapter One

Russia's Foreign Policy Objectives under Putin

Henry Kissinger taught us that in relations among states the crucial variables are both capability and will. Unless a state has the will to dominate other states as well as the capability to do so, those states have little reason to worry. Although Russian President Vladimir Putin has denied trying to re-constitute the Soviet Union, his actions show quite vividly that he has the will to dominate the states that were under Moscow's control as part of the USSR. Soon after taking office in 2000, he asserted that those states consti-tute a Russian sphere of influence that is strategically vital to the nation.[1] Utterances by officials who speak for him have echoed that perspective. When he temporarily left the presidency to assume the post of Prime Minis-ter, his anointed successor, Dmitri Medvedev,[2] promptly announced that Russia had "privileged interests" in the countries of the Former Soviet Un-ion, especially those where numerous Russian ethnics still live—many with Russian passports. More recently Foreign Minister Sergei Lavrov claimed "unique relations" with the countries of the Commonwealth of Independent States (CIS) based on what some Russian nationalist theorists have termed "civilizational unity."[3]

That sense of unity is expressed in the phrase "Near Abroad," which has been widely used in the Russian media almost from the moment the USSR collapsed at the end of 1991. The term is usually meant to refer to all the newly independent states that constituted the Soviet Union together with Russia. By distinguishing between those particular states and all others in the international system, this concept reflects a view held by most Russians, namely that the countries that had been part of the USSR, and before that, of the Russian Empire, are and should be objects of special interest, and the Russians who reside there are likewise objects of special concern to Russia. From the outset there has been considerable disagreement among Russians as to the policy implications of such interest and concern: should the Russian Federation respect the independence of these countries and their right to pursue whatever foreign and domestic policies they desire, or should it strive to bring them under its influence and protection? Russian liberals have argued for the former course, as have many economists and others who might be described as "realists," owing to their focus on Russia's limited resources. These realists believe that Russia should use its resources to invest in new infrastructure and modernize its economy, rather than to attempt to extend its influence and protection beyond its borders. Russian nationalists, on the other hand, have maintained that Moscow has a sacred obligation to reunite the states of the CIS under Russian tutelage and protect their kinsmen in those states from discrimination at the hands of non-Russian governments. Moreover, in their view, Russian foreign policy must aim at the restoration of a strong Russian state, both internally and externally. Russia is destined to be a great power, and Moscow's foreign policy should focus on restoring that status. The area of the world in which it is most critical to assert Russia's power is the Near Abroad, from which the most acute threats to Russia and Russians are likely to emanate and which has historically constituted Russia's sphere of influence. While not embracing all the tenets of Russian nationalism, after he became President, Putin seemed increasingly to sympathize with this latter perspective. Accordingly, observers have noted the intimate connection between Moscow's two major foreign policy goals under the Putin presidency: restoration of Russia's great power status and maintenance of its dominant influence in states around its border to guard against potential security threats. [4]

It is true that an important official policy document, the Foreign Policy Concept of the Russian Federation, published in July 2008, endorsed a vision of a Greater Europe in which Russia and its western neighbors would be merely constituent parts with equal status. This document called for a Euro-Atlantic security partnership "from Vancouver to Vladivostok." However, if Putin ever seriously entertained this idea, he unquestionably abandoned it once it became clear that Western governments desired an "Atlanticist" approach to such a partnership, in which their political institutions would predominate. [5] From Putin's perspective, democratic "color revolutions" like those in Georgia (2003) and Ukraine (2004), applauded by the West, constitute an existential threat to his power and that of the wealthy oligarchs and associates from the former secret police ("*siloviki*") who support him. These uprisings also have the potential to lead to NATO membership for countries in the Near Abroad and therefore endanger Russia's national security.

A more recent version of Russia's Foreign Policy Concept better conveys Putin's foreign policy goals. It emphasizes the importance of "consolidating Russia's position as an influential center of power in the modern world."[6] In Putin's view, Russia's relationships with its neighbors will play a critical role in realizing this end. Putin has come to embrace the vision of post-Soviet Russia's most influential Foreign Minister, Yevgeny Primakov.[7] According to that vision, the dominant trend in today's international system is increasing multipolarity. In this emerging world order the United States and the Atlantic Alliance will no longer play the dominant role they enjoyed in the decades since World War II. Other centers of power are rising to challenge Western military power, economic dominance and ideological influence. Russia should exploit and advance this trend toward a multipolar world. The Russian Federation is itself one such center of power, but the alliances Russia is able to construct will further enhance its global influence. Some of these alliances may be far-flung: the BRICS (Brazil/Russia/India/China/South Africa) constitute one such alliance. Even more important for Putin are those which are based in Russia's neighborhood. In Putin's eyes, the Collective Security Treaty Organization (CSTO), modeled on NATO, and the Eurasian Economic Union (EaEU),[8] modeled on the EU, both have the potential to compete with their western counterparts and enhance Russia's power and status as a global actor. Putin's intention is that both alliances will expand beyond the confines of the former Soviet Union. Thus he offered observer status in the CSTO to Afghanistan and Serbia. Both these states, which are quite friendly, to Russia, accepted. The EaEU, Putin anticipates, will grow into a "powerful supra-national union" of sovereign states, uniting members' economies, legal systems and military capabilities. Someday, he hopes, it will serve as a bridge between the EU and the United States.[9] Putin has been discussing free trade agreements between the EaEU and more than thirty states. Vietnam, Egypt, Iran, and Serbia have concluded such agreements; Thailand, Israel, New Zealand, Tunisia, and Turkey have expressed interest, as has China. However, the majority of states in the Near Abroad remain outside it, and China has not been admitted to its customs union.

Sometimes described as "Primakov's brainchild," the Shanghai Cooperation Organization, which includes China, India, and Pakistan, as well as four of the five Central Asian states, was founded in 2001. It has the most potential of all Russia's neighborhood alliances for enhancing its power on the world stage. Its purpose is to promote both economic and security cooperation, with the security threats its members face defined as "terrorism, separatism and extremism." The more Russia feels pressured by Western sanctions, the more it has turned to the SCO for support. Since 2014 Russia's ties with China have been expanding steadily, and the SCO has been playing an important role in fortifying those ties. In February 2014, the two Asian giants concluded a $400 billion gas deal and are now cooperating under the aegis of the SCO to protect the pipelines that will transport the gas from Central Asian insurgents. After concluding the deal, Putin declared that the unipolar world order was over.[10] He responded to the recent decision by the G-7 to deny Russia's readmission by declaring that he was in no hurry for his country to be reinstated because it already belongs to a more important economic grouping. The G-7 represents fewer people, encompasses less territory, and has less economic weight than the SCO, he asserted.[11]

Putin's approach to his neighbors has helped to strengthen his hold on power at home. For a long time Putin's actions in Russia's neighborhood have been largely (although not universally) applauded at home. A poll in 2017 reported 74 percent of the Russian people trusted him and supported his policies vis-à-vis the Near Abroad.[12] After a campaign that focused largely on his invasion and occupation of Crimea, he was re-elected to a fourth term in 2018 by a similar percentage of those voting.

PUTIN AND THE EMERGENCE OF RUSSIAN ASSERTIVISM

By the end of Putin's first term as President (2000–2004), it began to appear that he had rejected the possibility of cooperating with NATO and was increasingly wary of the political and economic role the EU might play in the former Soviet sphere. The admission of the Baltic States to NATO in 2004 and Western support for Ukraine's Orange Revolution later that year alarmed and infuriated him. Russia's revenues from oil and gas had begun to rise markedly by then after a long period of extremely low prices, and this probably strengthened Putin's resolve to prevent, resist and counter both NATO expansion and democratic revolution in Russia's neighborhood.

By 2006–2007 Russian foreign policy had begun to reflect a new assertivism. This involved taking whatever steps, at home and abroad, that were necessary to prevent Western interference in Russia's domestic politics and the domestic politics of the states in the Near Abroad. In 2007 Putin put the West on notice that such interference was unacceptable and would not be tolerated.[13] Assertivism also entailed strengthening Russia's national defense, and Putin announced his determination to do just that.[14] Western moves that were perceived as aggressive—such as NATO's plans to deploy components of a new missile defense system in Poland and the Czech Republic—would be met with new Russian weapons, Putin warned, and Russia would suspend participation in the Treaty on Conventional Armed Forces in Europe.[15] There would also be retaliation for any further NATO expansion, which Moscow regarded as a violation of assurances Russia had received from Manfred Werner, Secretary General of NATO in 1990.[16]

Strengthening Russia's position in the Near Abroad was a crucial component of Putin's new assertivism. He was aided by the fact that the consensus among Kremlin policymakers and most of the public in favour of Russia's dominant role in the now independent parts of the former Soviet Union appeared to be intensifying. Moscow began to rely heavily on energy exports as a weapon to be deployed against neighbors who defied or offended the Kremlin. Prices on these exports were raised to uncooperative states, and failure to pay or other perceived misdeeds resulted in the cut-off of supplies, sometimes in the dead of winter.[17] Moscow began to employ cyberwarfare in the form of attacks on computer systems in neighboring states: Estonia, Georgia, and even friendly Kyrgyzstan became targets in 2007–2009.[18] Another means to establish dominance, Putin hoped, would be pipeline construction linking Russia to former Soviet countries that exported energy. He tried to convince Kazakhstan, Turkmenistan, and Uzbekistan to increase their exports of energy through both new and established Russian pipelines, rather than through the Baku-Ceyhan pipeline being built by the United States through Azerbaijan and Georgia.

It was at this time that Putin also began to focus on the process of Eurasian economic integration described above. This process began in the 1990s but had made little headway, producing little in the way of economic integration. In 2007 Putin persuaded Belarus and Kazakhstan to join Russia in a new customs union which the President hoped would ultimately embrace all former Soviet states, thereby countering the EU and preventing its further expansion eastward.[19] At the same time, the establishment of closer relations with pro-Russian separatist regions on the territory of other former Soviet states became a foreign policy focus. The use of force, if necessary to prevent more of those states from joining NATO, began to figure in Russian military planning, and concerns over Georgia's growing cooperation with and possible imminent accession to NATO led Russia to invade in 2008. Lessons learned from problems Russian forces encountered in that operation resulted in a much smoother operation in Crimea in 2014.

Military integration of the Near Abroad also assumed an important place on Putin's newly assertivist agenda. Like economic integration, this process, too, had begun in the 1990s with the creation of a security alliance that initially included five post-Soviet states other than the Russian Federation.[20] Putin hoped to expand this alliance to include more members, enhance and intensify military cooperation and conduct large scale annual military exercises. As a result of Putin's efforts, the Collective Security Treaty Organization (CSTO) was formed in 2002, and such exercises were institutionalized. The organization now includes a rapid reaction force that can help to quell rebellion or unrest and thereby keep the peace (see Chapter 3). Russia appears to assume it may deploy this force as it sees fit on the territory of member states of the alliance, although it has failed to convince the UN to endorse the deployment of the force in non-member states in the Near Abroad, including Ukraine. Putin also convinced the other CSTO members to give the Russian Federation the right to veto the establishment of new foreign military bases on their soil. By 2019 this assertivism in Russia's neighborhood, combined with Russian activities in the Middle East, had succeeded in convincing most (75 percent) Russians that their country was indeed a "superpower."[21]

PUTIN'S POLICY TOWARD THE NEAR ABROAD: OTHER VIEWPOINTS

Two experienced observers have expressed the opinion that under Putin Russia "has reorganized its entire foreign and domestic policy in order to pursue a single objective, namely, the establishment of a new kind of union comprised of former Soviet republics and headed by Russia itself . . . a geopolitical edifice to include politics, security, and culture."[22] If these authors are correct, then Putin's ambitions are not being met. However, achieving dominance does not require the construction of a new "geopolitical edifice" or a reconstituted Soviet-style political union. We see no sign that Putin is seeking such a union.

A recent book has argued that a "Russian re-imperialization trajectory" in territories where Russian compatriots reside aims at "protection and finally . . . annexation."[23] We disagree and doubt that there is a general strategy of annexation. As we were taught, foreign policy among sovereign states depends on both will *and* capability. No leader of the Russian Federation has voiced the will to annex the states of the "Near Abroad," though possibly in future some small areas with large Russian populations, such as Abkhazia and South Ossetia in Georgia, may prefer to adhere to the Russian Federation rather than to retain their current status as independent states recognized only by Russia and a handful of other countries around the world. Putin has denied any designs on Eastern Ukraine, and we find that credible. The retaking of Crimea, where there are a majority of Russian compatriots, was motivated, we believe, primarily by a desire to retain critical naval assets in the Black Sea port of Sevastopol. No further territorial expansion is necessary to support Putin's domestically popular effort to restore Russia as a major world power. Moreover, his country does not have the necessary material capability to expand. Crimea already costs the Kremlin a considerable sum to pay pensions and improve health and education within the present Russian Federation, where Putin's political standing is at stake. Annexation of the provinces of Luhansk and Donetz in eastern Ukraine would be even more expensive. Obviously, any military move on the Baltic States would risk encountering NATO collective defense, as the Russian President knows.

At the other end of the spectrum of views regarding Russia's ambitions in the Near Abroad is the writing of Stephen Kotkin, a distinguished historian. In a lead article published in *Foreign Affairs* in 2016 Kotkin wrote: "Apart from a few military bases Russia is out of Central Asia." Somewhat later in the same piece, however, he conceded: "But except for the Baltics, all [Central Asian states] are economically dependent on Russia to various degrees."[24] We believe military and economic connections, not to mention longtime cultural commonality, give Russia very considerable influence in all these states, despite their nominal independence. Russia has no intention of leaving Central Asia or any other portion of the Near Abroad. The question is how much influence or control Moscow will seek, what will it do to obtain it, and under what circumstances. That will depend on geography and political choices on all sides, as we show in Chapters 4–6.

PUTIN'S OBJECTIVES IN THE NEAR ABROAD

We have argued that in Putin's view, asserting Russian dominance in the Near Abroad is an essential component of his quest to restore the country's great power status. He has had four specific objectives in dealing with the Near Abroad. To appraise the success of Russia's efforts to dominate his neighbors, one must consider the degree to which his pursuit of those objectives has enhanced, or at least reinforced, the power of the Russian state.

His objectives, as evidenced by Kremlin statements and actions, appear to be (1) *preventing radical democratic regime change in the Near Abroad that might weaken the domestic stability of his increasingly authoritarian regime and thereby undermine his power.*

There seems to be an ideological dimension, as well as personal ambition, inherent in this effort. Putin appears to believe that unfettered democratic competition and debate, as well as decentralization of power, are bad for Russia and perhaps for any society because they lead to chaos, disorganization, and paralysis. The Russian president has been significantly influenced by the ideas of his one-time ideological mentor, Vladislav Surkov, author of the concept of "sovereign" or "managed" democracy.[25] Surkov first publicly articulated this concept in a speech to a conference of United Russia, the political party created in 2001 to mobilize support for Putin. While the meaning of the phrase has never been authoritatively established, Surkov seems to have envisioned a centralized political system, dominated by (although not necessarily limited to) a single party, which would "manage" the operation of democratic institutions to ensure the well-being and prosperity of society. Such a system would be a "sovereign democracy," in that it would bolster the power of the state, both internally and externally. Putin appears to have embraced this concept wholeheartedly after the "color revolutions" in Georgia and Ukraine in 2003–2004. He followed Surkov's advice to establish a mass youth movement (called Nashi) that would be loyal to the state, especially to its president, and combat their critics. Founded in 2005 in the aftermath of Ukraine's "Orange Revolution," Nashi was designed to serve as an "anti-Orange" force of tens of thousands of youth trained to be ready to take to the streets to intimidate demonstrators and forcibly disband any antigovernment demonstrations that might occur in the Russian Federation. Starting in 2006, Putin also initiated a series of measures to suppress actual or potential dissent within the Russian Federation, eliminating independent television stations, expelling NGO's that received funding from abroad, sponsoring legislation that severely penalized participation in demonstrations, forcibly breaking up such demonstrations when they did occur, and jailing organizers. Very likely such measures have discouraged political protest at home.

However, to prevent democratic regime change in Russia, Putin has thought it necessary to ensure that color revolutions would not take place on Russia's borders, from which they might spill over into Russia itself. That has been his primary objective in the Near Abroad since 2004, when a sustained popular uprising toppled the pro-Russian government in Ukraine.

Putin's efforts to prevent democratic regime change abroad have not been entirely successful, but the spillover effects of revolution in the Near Abroad have been minimal—his ultimate objective. In 2005 Kyrgyzstan became the scene of mass demonstrations against a corrupt authoritarian ruler (Askar Akayev) hitherto backed by Russia. Putin was able to limit the damage by quickly befriending his successor, Kurmanbek Bakiyev. When Bakiyev defied Moscow by renewing his contract with the United States for use of Manas Airbase in 2009, Putin appears to have welcomed his overthrow and may even have helped to precipitate the rioting that led to his downfall and replacement by a more compliant leader the following year.[26] One widely respected observer described Putin's actions as "a critical piece of Russia's overall plan to resurge into the former Soviet sphere."[27]

Much more was at stake for Russia in the "Euromaidan Revolution" of 2013–2014 in Ukraine.[28] In contrast with remote Kyrgyzstan, on the border with China, Ukraine is a critical buffer state between the Russian Federation and the newly expanded NATO alliance. While Bishkek, Kyrgyzstan's capital, is almost two thousand miles from Moscow, Kiev is less than five hundred miles away, and Russia's cultural, linguistic, demographic, and economic ties with Ukraine are far closer and more significant. Ukraine had been a key component of Russia's plans for a Eurasian economic union, which is integral to Putin's quest to restore his country's great power status. It was Ukraine's overwhelming vote for independence in 1991 that precipitated the collapse of the USSR.

What initially triggered the protests that began the revolution in Ukraine was the decision by that country's then-President Viktor Yanukovich to refrain from signing a laboriously negotiated association and free trade agreement with the EU and establish closer economic ties with Russia instead.[29] As the protests escalated, gradually becoming violent, nervous Russian officials pressured the Ukrainian government to do what whatever was necessary to crush the rioting and reportedly began dispatching on-the-scene advisers to the Ukrainian police. However, the ensuing police attacks on the demonstrators only resulted in an escalation of the violence.[30] As Moscow saw it, Western politicians and organizations were responsible for the crisis because of the role they played in encouraging the unrest. The behavior of the opposition constituted an attempt to stage a coup against Ukraine's legitimate government "by Kalashnikov-toting people roaming Kiev in black masks."[31] A senior adviser to Putin accused the United States of training and arming opposition fighters on the grounds of the U.S. embassy. Hardline Russian nationalists claimed that the uprising was a Western plot to extract Ukraine from Russia's sphere of influence. Putin insisted that Russia had guaranteed Ukrainian sovereignty in a 1994 agreement and now was obliged to fulfill its pledge.[32] When Yanukovich fled to Russia and the Parliament voted to remove him, Russia declared this action was illegal. Following a formal request by the deposed Ukrainian leader, Russian troops occupied Crimea and took up positions in the south and east of the country, helping pro-Russian counter-protestors establish what would become in effect, independent states in Donetsk and Luhansk.[33]

Once again Putin failed to prevent the democratic revolution he so dreaded. However, his response to events in Ukraine were wildly popular at home, where a controlled media relayed only the Kremlin's evaluation of those events. The Russian president thus succeeded in strengthening not only his regime's hold on power, but also his country's position in the Near Abroad. We discuss these efforts at greater length in Chapters 4 and 5.

Both to prevent Russia's neighbors from supporting alternatives to Putin's rule, as well as to protect the country against a cross-border military assault, another critical Russian objective in the Near Abroad is that of (2) *excluding NATO from areas on its borders*. At the Munich Conference on Security Policy in 2007, President Putin famously said that NATO expansion "represents a serious provocation that reduces the level of mutual trust."[34] Placement of NATO missiles or troops in areas on or near Russia's borders would complicate Russian defense, which traditionally depends on strategic depth. Russia's permanent representative to NATO in Brussels warned that accession of Georgia or Ukraine would put Europe in a serious confrontation with his country. However, at a NATO conference in Bucharest, Romania, in April 2008, the George W. Bush administration defied Putin's warning and proposed admitting both Georgia and Ukraine to NATO. Although immediate membership was rejected by France and Germany, NATO members did issue a special communiqué assuring the Georgians they could join once they had met requirements for membership. Not surprisingly, this overture put the Putin government on notice, and some four months later Russian forces invaded Georgia.

Russian diplomats remember that former U.S. Secretary of State James Baker promised that reunification of Germany would *not* lead to NATO expansion eastward. Strobe Talbott, former Ambassador-at-Large and special assistant to the Secretary of State in the administration of U.S. President Bill Clinton, admitted to one of us at a luncheon at Indiana University that, yes, Baker had made this promise, the State Department had a record of it, but it was "not an official commitment of the US government." Clearly the Russians felt betrayed anyway.

Quite obviously, though, Russia's objective of excluding NATO from states near its borders has not been fully achieved. President Clinton pushed NATO membership through for Poland in 1999.[35] Lithuania, Latvia, and Estonia received this status under President G.W. Bush in 2004. All these countries are adjacent to Russian territory. Thus NATO's collective security promise embodied in Article 5, as applied to members on Russia's western border, poses a serious strategic threat today.

In fact, NATO has also achieved a presence, albeit limited, in much of the rest of the Near Abroad. Following the Al-Qaeda attack on the World Trade Center and the Pentagon, Putin acquiesced when American airmen were stationed in Uzbekistan from 2001 to 2005, followed by German airmen on behalf of NATO after that. Islam Karimov, the late President of Uzbekistan, allowed NATO to use air routes to Afghanistan over his territory to supply alliance forces from the north via the Termez airport transit point, instead of mostly through Pakistan. NATO planes were allowed to land in Turkmenistan en route from Western Europe to Afghanistan. The United States also enjoyed the use of an airbase in Kyrgyzstan, as we have mentioned, and employed servicemen in Uzbekistan to assist NATO's Afghanistan operations. Turkmenistan, Uzbekistan, and Kazakhstan all provided land-based delivery corridors for use by NATO in transporting non-lethal cargo from Western Europe to Afghanistan.[36] All these NATO activities in Central Asia have now been terminated, though all five countries in this region continue to cooperate with NATO in various ways. Kazakhstan even holds annual military exercises (dubbed "Steppe Eagle") with NATO contingents aimed at ensuring interoperability of NATO and Kazakhstani forces.[37]

NATO has substantially reinforced its activities in Ukraine since the Russian annexation of Crimea in 2014. The alliance provides strategic advice; senior Ukrainian military officers participate regularly in NATO training courses, and NATO officers are working with Ukrainian forces to enhance their ability to defend the country. Ukraine has officially cancelled its "non-bloc" status, and the Ukrainian parliament has adopted legislation declaring that membership in NATO is a foreign and security policy objective.[38] As a candidate, the country's newest President, Volodymyr Zelensky, affirmed that he regarded Putin as an enemy and repeatedly stated that he favored joining NATO.[39]

Georgia's ties with NATO are even closer than Ukraine's. The newest government has openly declared its aspiration to join, and the alliance has repeatedly endorsed that goal. NATO advisers work closely with the Georgian Defense Ministry and General Staff. Periodic exercises involving NATO and Georgian forces take place on Georgian territory, NATO troops provide anti-terrorism training, and sustained cooperation occurs in many areas.[40]

If Putin has been unable to keep NATO out of the Near Abroad, he has managed to prevent the accession of any other states since 2004. This is undoubtedly a result of his manifested willingness to use force to prevent any other former Soviet state from joining. Despite repeated professions of interest in doing so by both Ukraine and Georgia, and despite the fact that more than a decade has passed since these countries were promised they could do so in the future, the alliance has declined to take that step.[41] After the Russian invasion of Georgia in 2008 and dispatch of forces into Ukraine in 2014, Moscow's threats to take actions of the same sort in the future has been completely credible. The continued presence of large numbers of Russian troops in or very near the borders of these countries has served as a powerful deterrent to their admission.[42] These matters are explored further in Chapter 5.

All countries seek to ensure their sovereignty by controlling their borders. A great power will attempt to accomplish this objective by erecting and protecting a sphere of influence surrounding it. Another vital interest of Moscow in the Near Abroad is (3) *interdicting the flow of Islamist terrorists, arms, and drugs* to prevent their entry into the Russian Federation. Islamists from the Caucasus, Afghanistan, and beyond are active inside and around Russia's southern borders.[43] Some Central Asians have reportedly been radicalized on construction sites within Russia, and jihadist recruiters have been arrested in St. Petersburg.[44] In 2016 it was estimated that four thousand Russian citizens and some three thousand from neighboring countries had gone to Syria and Iraq to join ISIS.[45] With ISIS territory now nearly eliminated, some of the frustrated and experienced survivors are trying to return to make trouble in Russia and its neighborhood, as well as in Western Europe.[46]

In addition, the resurgence of Afghanistan's Taliban since 2015 may allow Islamists to penetrate Uzbekistan, Tajikistan, Turkmenistan, and Kyrgyzstan, and even the Muslim-majority areas within the Russian Federation. There they might well make common cause with hitherto suppressed opponents of the Central Asian regimes and thus threaten Russian interests. To ensure against such a possibility, Russia has recently been making overtures to the Taliban. Some top U.S. commanders even claim that Moscow has been arming them.[47]

The vulnerability of Russia's southern border is especially clear in the Caucasus region, composed of small territories that are part of or adjacent to the Near Abroad. Caucasian terrorists, funded by foreign Islamists, have repeatedly launched attacks within Russia. Moscow twice fought to suppress Chechen separatism, much of it fueled by Islamism. Putin spearheaded the second of these campaigns, becoming, as one observer has noted, "obsessed with Chechnya" because the conflict there threatened to lead to further disintegration of the Russian Federation. This was Putin's worst nightmare.[48] Even if Chechnya is pacified for now, this is not true of all the other small Muslim-majority areas in the North Caucasus.[49] Seventy Russian policemen and others were killed in "increasingly ungovernable" Dagestan and Ingushetia in 2009.[50] Two years later, car bombs killed a Russian policeman and wounded dozens of others in the capital of Dagestan, the largely Muslim and ethnically diverse Russian Federation republic in the North Caucasus region.[51] Violence against Russians in these largely Muslim republics within the Russian Federation has been almost continuous since then. Moscow itself has numerous resident Caucasians and Central Asians who may be drawn into violence, as probably was the case in a lethal bomb attack on the St. Petersburg metro in April 2017.[52]

The flow of narcotics to Russia's millions of addicts, many of whom are victims of HIV, has not abated. On the contrary, the problem is growing, owing to a very substantial increase in opium production in Afghanistan since 2015. Expansion of the Eurasian Economic Union (EaEU) has exacerbated the problem by reducing controls along the Russia-Kyrgyzstan border.[53] Curbing this flow is a key motivation of Russian involvement in Tajikistan, where the drug-related illness is rising fast. At the same time, Moscow's efforts to reduce drug trafficking enable it to strengthen its security cooperation with Central Asia. Support for Tajikistan's activities in this sphere helps to legitimize Russia's projection of power into that country. President Emomali Rahmon explained Russia's recent upgrade of its military base there as necessary for Moscow to assist in suppression of the drug trade. Such arguments may help Putin convince hitherto reluctant Uzbekistan to expand its security cooperation with Russia as well.[54] The role of these illegal cross-border flows and Russia's efforts to control them in its relations with its southern neighbors is explored further in Chapter 4.

If suppression of democratic challenges to Putin's rule and thus to the strength and power of the Russian state is Putin's greatest concern, securing the support of wealthy oligarchs who can help to enlarge government coffers and thereby keep him in office is likewise critical from his perspective. Russia's activities in the Near Abroad are vital to this endeavor: (4) *keeping the money flowing to his supporters* is, therefore, the last of his important objectives there.

Some of Russia's top elite, especially (but not exclusively) among the so-called *siloviki* (former security personnel), have made fabulous incomes by taking their cut of the country's wealth of raw materials, including those imported from neighboring countries. Both transit fees from oil and gas pipelines over Russian territory and government contracts from activities in the Near Abroad are extremely important in enriching this group of fifty or sixty individuals and thereby keeping them loyal to Putin. Prime Minister Medvedev provides the most notorious example of enrichment. While Russia in 2016 had seventy billionaires, according to *Forbes* magazine, this was three dozen fewer than in 2014, probably reflecting the decline in oil and gas and other rents.[55] Putin has a strong incentive to help his wealthy supporters retain and expand their fortunes, and his actions in the Near Abroad can help.

In Soviet times Russia was able to obtain an unlimited share of the oil and natural gas from Central Asia at prices permitting profitable resale in Europe. But now the situation in the oil and gas sector is changing markedly, and will probably continue to do so for an indefinite period ahead. Russia's oil and gas companies, once the sole purchasers of Central Asian energy, have been successfully challenged by Chinese customers. Turkmenistan, Kazakhstan, and Uzbekistan have allowed gas pipelines to be built by Chinese workers to supply the People's Republic's considerable energy needs. Azerbaijan and Georgia agreed to construction of the Baku-Tblisi-Ceyhan (BTC) oil pipeline from the Caspian Sea to the Turkish port on the Mediterranean, with the encouragement of American officials. This bypasses the Russian Federation altogether. All this competition has meant that Russian companies must pay up for supplies, and the profits from transit fees of the Russian oligarchs who run them have diminished.

Russian energy companies also face growing competition as suppliers of energy to European markets. Shale gas supplies have increased worldwide, so final cash prices to Russian consumers in Europe have declined to new lows that are likely to remain. This cuts deeply into the oligarchs' profits. Russia has had to construct new and expensive underwater lines under the Black and Baltic Seas to its customers. As a consequence of weaker demand in Europe, as well as sanctions imposed after the invasion of Crimea, Russia's once dreamed-of South Stream pipeline to Bulgaria and on through Serbia, Hungary, and Slovenia to Austria, was cancelled in December 2014.[56] By this point, both the EU and the Russian Federation were prepared to abandon the plan. However, the cancellation was a tremendous blow to everyone in Moscow: to Putin, who was fighting to maintain Russia's share of the European gas market; to Gazprom, which had already invested heavily in the project and stood to reap huge profits from it; and to Gazprom's CEO Alexey Miller, a Putin protégé who would have amassed considerable personal wealth from the undertaking. This development has made access to Central Asian gas and the ability to transport it to world markets all the more important to the Russian government—and to Putin personally.[57]

Proceeds from the sale and distribution of gas and oil are only the largest source of profit to be obtained from the Near Abroad. Central Asian producers of cotton now sell their crops at world prices, not those lower ones set by Moscow. Nonetheless, Moscow insiders benefit from the profitable sale of gold and caviar transported from the Near Abroad through Russia to the world market.[58]

Sales of Russian products to the Near Abroad are also major sources of revenues for Russia's oligarchs. Russia is the second largest arms exporter in the world, after the United States, but two of Moscow's best customers—China and India—are rapidly increasing their own production. Austerity forced by lower energy prices makes the sale of arms to the militaries of Russia's former Soviet neighbors, even if at lower prices, all the more important. Kazakhstan, Azerbaijan, and Belarus are now among Russia's top customers. Some weapons, such as torpedoes, are tested in the Near Abroad.

As the reselling of the resources of the Near Abroad has become less lucrative, Russia has tried new ways to profit. Protectionism is one means, as it increases the market for Russian production. The newly established Eurasian Economic Union has put up tariffs to protect the Russian market in Kazakhstan and elsewhere in the Near Abroad from European, South Asian, and East Asian competitors, which can offer cheaper and better goods. Major construction projects within Russia's sphere of influence, especially new energy infrastructure such as pipelines and power grids, but also roads and other civil engineering projects, provide huge corrupt benefits for individuals close to Putin.[59] Such patronage and wealth help support Putin and his associates and, indirectly, his rule.

We have tried to show in this introductory chapter that Putin's desire to recover Russia's status as a first-rate world player has been pursued, with considerable, although not unqualified success, by his policies in the expanse of the Near Abroad. These countries provide a kind of *cordon sanitaire* against radical democratic politics from without and within the Russian Federation. While NATO has established many ties in the Near Abroad, Western forces are to be found now only in the Baltic States. All the other neighbors cooperate in outlawing secessionist and Islamist militants and in combating drugs and arms smuggling. Russia's ruling group continues to reap profits from the country's investments and subsidized exports to surrounding countries. So all of Putin's four objectives in the Near Abroad have been satisfied at a fairly low cost—less than imperial rule would incur—permitting Putin to accept limited, and perhaps temporary, ventures in the outside world befitting a great power. Chapters 4–6 will provide more detailed treatments of what has developed under Putin's leadership in the Near Abroad: cheap cooperation in the south, protection or threats in the southwest, armed confrontation but avoidance of armed conflict in the northwest.

RUSSIA, CHINA, AND THE NEAR ABROAD

Russia's relationship with China is more complex than its relationship with any of its other neighbors. Accordingly, its objectives in dealing with China during the Putin presidency are also more contradictory. That complexity and those contradictions are nowhere more apparent than with regard to the Near Abroad.

China has been very helpful to Russia as a partner, assisting it in many ways in fortifying its great power status in a multipolar world—Putin's overall goal in foreign policy. China and Russia have shared common global aims in the Putin era: both are committed to ensuring respect for state sovereignty,[60] preventing regime change at home and abroad, and opposing Western intervention in the affairs of others (which both see as part of an illegitimate quest for Western hegemony and world dominance). As Putin's concern regarding the threat from NATO and rising American military spending has mounted, China's growing nuclear and conventional military challenge to the United States has undoubtedly been welcome. The People's Republic usefully diverts American resources and attention away from the European theater and Russia, and toward the western Pacific.[61] In the diplomatic sphere, China usually provides welcome backing for Russia's policy positions at the UN and around the world, generally in opposition to the positions of the United States or western governments generally. The two former Communist nations have stood together on a broad range issues, not merely the Russian annexation of Crimea,[62] but also the U.S. invasion of Iraq, sanctions on Iran and North Korea, intervention against Assad in the Syria Civil War, Syria's use of chemical weapons, the military junta in Myanmar, conflict in Zimbabwe, and most recently, the political situation in Venezuela.

Western sanctions on Russia since 2014 have made China an increasingly important economic partner. This has been especially true in the Arctic. Chinese capital and technology are helping Russia reduce the impact of constraints on Western investment in vital Russian energy projects and promising infrastructure construction to develop the Northern Sea Route.[63] But the partnership extends well beyond the Arctic. Since 2014, Russia has concluded major deals to sell natural gas and advanced weapons to China, and Chinese companies have made substantial investments in Russian petrochemical production, purchased stakes in Russian oilfields and liquefied natural gas projects, agreed to help finance construction of a major oil pipeline and put money into large farms near the Sino-Russian border.[64] Gazprom is building a vast pipeline to supply gas from east Siberian fields to Chinese consumers, while trade between the two countries rose 15 percent in 2018.[65]

In the Near Abroad China and Russia have a mostly cooperative relationship at present. China supports Russia's anti-democratic agenda, not only at home, but in the Near Abroad as well. The two powers share a strong desire to maintain stable authoritarian rule in Central Asia and suppress any manifestations of Islamism in the region or emanating from there.[66] China avoids criticizing Russia's efforts to control the foreign policies of the former Soviet states, evincing no disapproval of its use of its "energy weapon" or armed force to achieve its objectives. Both governments are committed to strengthening the Shanghai Cooperation Organization and thus, in Putin's view, to forging a new pole of power to contest Western aspirations to dominate the international system. Most importantly, Beijing's public rhetoric has not contested Russia's claims to a privileged sphere of influence in the Near Abroad, and China generally refrains from attempting to influence foreign policymaking by Central Asian governments on matters unrelated to economics.

Nonetheless, there are significant elements of competition between Russia and China in the Near Abroad. These have the potential to expand and in the future even dominate the interactions between these two neighbors. China is increasingly competing with Russia for markets in Central Asia, and Russia has therefore declined to include China in the Eurasian Economic Union it has sponsored. China is clearly winning this competition. For the first two decades after the collapse of the Soviet Union, Russia was the primary importer of Central Asian gas and oil, sending refined fuels back to the region. Road, rail and pipeline connections established in Soviet times facilitated this exchange. But in the 2000s China began to make major investments in those areas, and its imports have soared as a result. By 2017 China's trade with Central Asia was almost double that of Russia ($30 billion, as opposed to $18.6 billion annually). The vast resources of this part of the Near Abroad are now going to China, far more than to Russia. A major purpose of the EaEU has been to combat this drastic shift in trade patterns. But while Russia is exerting pressure on its neighbors to join that organization, China is trying to make the Shanghai Cooperation Organization the basis of regional economic integration.[67] Arguably, Russia's efforts to extend membership in SCO to additional countries, such as India and Pakistan, may be intended to counter China's growing influence in that organization and ensure that it does not compete with the EaEU. Russia has blocked China's economic initiatives in SCO, such as its attempts to create a Regional Development Bank or an Anti-Crisis Fund.[68] China would be the chief lender in such an organization, thereby deepening still further its involvement in the economies of Central Asia.

The competition for trade may soon be extended to Europe. The transportation infrastructure China has built in Central Asia is intended not only to exploit that region's resources, but to enable China to reach markets in Europe as well. While China has long touted the advantages to Russia of extending that infrastructure through its territory as part of its Belt and Road Initiative (BRI), Moscow has been wary of such efforts. One reason for this resistance may be the access such development would offer China to European markets.[69]

Until very recently, China has not sought to establish a military position in Central Asia, but that could be changing. The more extensive its economic involvement, the more it may desire a larger security presence there to protect its interests. At the same time, its growing concern regarding terrorist operations in Afghanistan and infiltration of terrorists across its borders already seems to be leading it to greater military involvement in the region. It has built an extensive network of roads along Tajik/Afghan border. These appear to be used for little other than patrols by Chinese military vehicles. A Chinese military base along that border is under construction, and China has sought to establish a new security partnership, the Quadrilateral Cooperation and Coordination Mechanism, involving Tajikistan, Afghanistan, and Pakistan. Russia has not been invited to join and is reportedly very unhappy with these efforts.[70] Elsewhere in the world, most notably in Southeast Asia, substantial Chinese loans and investments have been followed by pressure to provide military facilities.[71] Generous Chinese economic aid to Sub-Saharan Africa has been followed by military aid, cooperation, and training programs. China's share of African arms purchases doubled after the Belt and Road Initiative was proclaimed. The People's Republic has recently established a China Africa Defense and Security Forum, which has been described as an emerging "China-centric, pan-African defense organization." China has built a military base in Djibouti and appears to be seeking to build one in West Africa as well.[72] Such developments are not inevitable in Central Asia, but they are certainly possible, and Russia would be likely to regard them as a significant challenge to its position in the Near Abroad. Insofar as control of the Near Abroad is crucial to Putin's quest for great power status, China's new economic dominance of Central Asia already serves as a constraint on Putin's ability to realize his central foreign policy goal. Should that dominance extend into the political and military spheres, the challenge to Russia would be even more substantial.

Chapter 7 explores the complex relationship between Russia and its largest neighbor. We examine the dramatic change in that relationship precipitated by Putin's use of force to secure Russia's position in Ukraine, the interests and perspectives the two countries share, and the potential for conflict between them.

NOTES

1. Stephen Erlanger, "The World: Learning to Fear Putin's Gaze," *The New York Times*, February 25, 2001. Even when Putin has denied interest in reconstituting the USSR, he has emphasized that he seeks a very close relationship between Russia and the former Soviet states. "There is no talk of reforming the USSR in some form. . . . It would be naïve to restore or copy what has been abandoned in the past, but close integration on the basis of new values, politics, and the economy is the order of the day," he declared soon after taking office. Charles Clover and Isabel Gorst, "Putin urges creation of Eurasian Union," *Financial Times*, October 5, 2001.

2. At the end of his second term as President in 2008, Putin was barred by the provisions of the constitution then in effect from running for a third term. He therefore selected his protégé Medvedev to run in his stead. Andrei Tsygankov, among other observers, emphasizes that Medvedev's foreign policy positions differed in some important ways from those of Putin. *Russia's Foreign Policy*, 5th ed. (Lanham, MD: Roman & Littlefield, 2019). We concur. However, his views on Russia's relationship with and role in the other newly independent states have been very much in line with Putin's.

3. The Commonwealth of Independent States (CIS) was created when the USSR disintegrated at the end of 1991. The organization was supposed to consist of the fifteen "republics" that had constituted the Soviet Union, but the Baltic States immediately asserted their complete lack of interest in joining. Turkmenistan and Ukraine were prepared to participate, but declined to ratify the organization's charter. Georgia withdrew from the CIS after Russia invaded portions of its territory in 2008, and Ukraine officially terminated its participation in 2018, following Russia's annexation of Crimea and prolonged military intervention in that country's eastern provinces.

4. See, for example, Dmitri Gorenberg, an expert on the Russian military, writing in Ponars Eurasia (quoted in *Russia Matters,* January 7, 2019).

5. Richard Sakwa, "Russian Neo-Revisionism and Dilemma of Eurasian Integration," in Roger E. Kanet and Matthew Sussex, eds., *Foreign Policy in a Contested Region* (Basingstroke, UK: Palgrave-Macmillan, 2015), 111–28. Sakwa believes that the Ukrainian crisis of 2014 ultimately ended what might have been a promising alternative. In his first two years in power (2000–2002), Putin may have briefly entertained this idea, but by 2003, he had dropped it.

6. Konstantin Volkov, *Nezavisimaya Gazeta*, December 5, 2016. CD **68**, no. 48–49: 17. (Elsewhere in this book "CD" stands for *Current Digest of the Russian Press* [East View, weekly]).

7. Samuel Ramani, "Yevgeny Primakov—The Ideological Godfather of Putinism," *Modern Diplomacy,* June 30, 2015.

8. The Collective Security Treaty Organization was formed by Russia with its closest allies in the Near Abroad (Belarus, Armenia, Tajikistan, Kazakhstan, and Kyrgyzstan) in 2002. The Eurasian Economic Union was established by Russia, Belarus, and Kazakhstan in 2014. Armenia and Kyrgyzstan joined the following year. See Chapter 3.

9. Jon Henley, "A Brief Primer on Vladimir Putin's Eurasian Dream," *The Guardian*, February 18, 2014.

10. Swagata Saha, "The Future of the SCO," *East Asia Forum*, February 17, 2014.

11. Andrew Higgins, "Putin Says He Would Welcome Meeting with Trump," *The New York Times*, June 10, 2018.

12. *The Economist,* September 23, 2017. His general performance approval declined somewhat by 2019.

13. Speech at Munich Security Conference, Feb. 10, 2007. http://en/Kremlin.ru/events/president/transcripts/24034.

14. Speeches to Council of the Russian Federation, May 10, 2006 and April 26, 2007.

15. "Russia in Defense Warning to U.S," *BBC News,* April 26, 2007; "Russia Suspends Arms Control Pact," *BBC News*, July 14, 2007.

16. Foreign Minister Sergei Lavrov, "NATO Expansion a Huge Mistake," Interfax, December 12, 2006. Werner reportedly said "The fact that we are prepared not to deploy a NATO army outside of German territory gives the Soviet Union a firm security guarantee." M. Laruelle and J. Radvanyi, *Understanding Russia* (Lanham, MD: Rowman & Littlefield, 2018), 107.

17. Russia had employed such methods since the collapse of the USSR, when they were unsuccessfully used against the Baltic states to dissuade them from joining NATO. However, they were now directed against many more of Russia's neighbors, with the result that many consumers in Western and Central Europe experienced shortages as well. Gabriel Collins, "Russia's Use of the 'Energy Weapon' in Europe," *Issue Brief,* Baker Institute for Public Policy, July 18, 2017.

18. Russia was punishing Estonia for its 2007 decision to move a Soviet war memorial to a more remote location. Damien McGuiness, "How a cyberattack transformed Estonia," *BBC News*, April 27, 2017. The attacks on Georgia came in the context of the Russian invasion and occupation in 2008. Kim Hart, "Longtime Battle Lines Are Recast in Russia and Georgia's Cyberwar," *Washington Post*, August 14, 2018. Kyrgyzstan had not yet resolved to shut down an American airbase, as Russia demanded. Christopher Rhoads, "Kyrgyzstan Knocked Offline," *Wall Street Journal,* January 28, 2009.

19. Irina Filatova, "Putin Calls for a New 'Eurasian Union of Former Soviet Countries," *The Moscow Times*, October 5, 2011. Many observers noted the potential political implications of such a project, sometimes exaggerating the likely outcome.

20. A Collective Security Treaty was signed in 1992 by Armenia, Kazakhstan, Kyrgyzstan, Tajikistan, and Uzbekistan, as well as the Russian Federation. Belarus joined the following year, but Uzbekistan subsequently withdrew.

21. *Russia Matters*, quoting a survey by the Levada Center in *The Moscow Times*, January 11, 2019. In 2005 it was only 30 percent.

22. S. Frederick Starr and S. Cornell eds., *Putin's Grand Strategy: the Eurasian Union and its Discontents.* (Washington, DC: Central Asia-Caucasus Institute and Silk Road Studies Program, 2014). Note that Starr and Cornell do not write "*all* the former Soviet Republics," as the Baltic states are now members of NATO. Whether Putin has a "grand strategy" or a single objective is doubtful, we think, but he does pursue tactics to achieve his main objectives, discussed below.

23. Agnia Grigas, *Beyond Crimea: The New Russian Empire* (New Haven, CT: Yale, 2016), 10. Grigas admits that annexation is a "possibility . . . which cannot be predicted or guaranteed," 27.

24. Stephen Kotkin, "Russia's Perpetual Geopolitics; Putin Returns to Historical Pattern," *Foreign Affairs* 95, no. 3 (May/June 2016): 2–9.

25. Vladislav Surkov, Speech to Conference of United Russia, February 22, 2006. Surkov and Putin reportedly are no longer close, but Putin may well have remained under the influence of Surkov's ideas.

26. The Russian media, by then largely controlled by the government, attacked Bakiyev, publicizing the corruption of his regime and its economic mismanagement. "Russian Mass Media Attack Bakiyev," *Eurasia Daily Monitor* 7, no. 63 (April 1, 2010). As control of the situation began to slip out of Bakiyev's hands, Moscow imposed duties on its energy exports to

the severely impoverished country, with the result that fuel and transport prices soared. "Kyrgyzstan: Is Russia Punishing Bakiyev?" *Eurasia Net*, April 6, 2010.

27. Lauren Goodrich, "Kyrgyzstan and the Russian Resurgence," *Stratfor*, April 13, 2010.

28. "Euromaidan" refers to Maidan Nezalezhnosti or Independence Square, where the protests that sparked the revolution began in November 2013.

29. "Ukraine Crisis," *BBC*, November 13, 2014.

30. Mark MacKinnon, "How Putin's Sochi Dream Was Shattered by Ukraine's Nightmare," *Globe and Mail*, February 22, 2014.

31. Dmitri Medvedev, quoted in "Vladimir Putin faces tough challenge as Ukraine turmoil unravels Russian designs," *Financial Express*, February 25, 2014.

32. "Ukraine Crisis: Putin Adviser Accuses U.S. of Meddling," BBC News, February 6, 2014.

33. "Lavrov: If West accepts coup-appointed Kiev government, it must accept a Russian Crimea," *RT News*, March 30, 2014; "Ousted Ukrainian President Asked for Russian Troops, Envoy Says," *NBC News*, Reuters, March 3, 2014; Tim Sullivan, "Russian Troops Take Over Crimea Region," *Associated Press*, March 1, 2014.

34. Vladimir Putin, speech to Munich Security Conference, February 10, 2007. http://en/Kremlin.ru/events/president/transcripts/24034.

35. Hungary and the Czech Republic were also admitted in 1999.

36. Turkmenistan's participation in these NATO activities was the most surprising, given that country's consistent commitment to neutrality. Bruce Palmer, "Turkmenistan: NATO Finds a New partner in Central Asia," *Radio Free Europe/Radio Liberty*, May 30, 2008.

37. North Atlantic Treaty Organization, *NATO's Relations with Central Asia*, February 22, 2016.

38. North Atlantic Treaty Organization, *Relations with Ukraine,* June 14, 2018.

39. Tom Parfitt, "Ukraine poll leader Volodymyr Zelensky sees Putin as an enemy," *The Times*," April 19, 2019; Steven Pifer (U.S. Ambassador to Ukraine 1998–2000), "How Ukraine's comedian-candidate could disappoint the Kremlin," *Washington Post*, April 19, 2019.

40. North Atlantic Treaty Organization, *Relations with Georgia,* June 22, 2018.

41. The promise was made at the NATO summit in Bucharest, Romania, in 2008.

42. Cf. the remarks by Lt. Gen. Ben Hodges, former commander of the U.S. Army in Europe, "NATO agreed Georgia would join. Why hasn't it happened?" PRI, March 27, 2019.

43. Russian Defense Minister Sergei Shogiu has said Islamic State militants from Iraq and Syria on the southern border with Afghanistan are stronger, must be identified by drones and defeated. *Interfax,* April 30, 2019. Quoted in *Russia Matters,* May 3, 2019.

44. *The Economist,* August 8, 2017. The "savage" metro bombing on April 3, 2017, has been blamed on an Uzbek from Osh, Kyrgyzstan, who had obtained Russian citizenship and residency. Similar attacks have occurred in Moscow's metro and airport.

45. Eric Schmitt, *The New York Times*, March 8, 2016; the source was the International Crisis Group. Persecuted at home, an estimated 2000 Tajiks have left to join the Islamic State. *The Economist,* September 23, 2017.

46. Alexander Bortnikov, Head of the Federal Security Service (FSB), Russia's principal security agency, recently declared that five thousand ISIS fighters were now deployed in northern Afghanistan and posed a direct threat to Russia's neighbors in Central Asia. Many are citizens of Central Asian countries seeking to cross back into those countries to spread their ideology, establish sleeper cells, and conduct acts of terrorism. Callum Paton, "Russia Spy Chief Warns 5000 ISIS Foreign Fighters Threaten Borders of FSU," *Newsweek*, May 21, 2019.

47. Dawood Azami, "Is Russia Arming the Taliban?" *BBC World Service*, April 2, 2018.

48. Michael Wines, "Why Putin Boils Over: Chechnya Is His Personal War," *The New York Times*, November 13, 2002. The observer Wines quotes was Alexander Rahr, a leading German expert on Russia who is personally acquainted with Putin.

49. All of Russia's five majority-Muslim areas are located in the North Caucasus, as is one other with a significant percentage of Muslims (defined as 10–50 percent in 2012). Seven other regions of the Russian Federation in the south or in the Urals have a significant percentage of Muslims.

50. *The Economist*, September 6, 2008. The situation in 2009 was tantamount to "civil war." *The Economist*, January 30, 2010. "Chechnya . . . is now a brutal dictatorship toying with *sharia* governance. The Muslim fundamentalist insurgence has spread to previously quiet Dagestan, Ingushetia, and Kabardino-Balkaria, while the Moscow Metro, planes, and an airport have been targets of devastating terrorist attacks." Leon Aron, "Russia's Deep Despair," *The New Republic*, March 24, 2011.

51. Olga Slobodchikova, "Russia: At Least 4 Are Killed by Car Bomb," *The New York Times*, September 28, Liberty, 2011.

52. "A Year After St. Petersburg Subway Blast, Russia Says Probe Almost Finished," Radio Free Europe/Radio April 3, 2018.

53. Sebastian Peyrouse, "Drug-Trafficking in Tajikistan: A Very Deep But Not Incurable Evil," *Georgetown Journal of International Affairs,* March 1, 2018.

54. Samuel Ramani, "Russia's Anti-Drug Crusade in Afghanistan," *The Diplomat*, December 28, 2017.

55. Kerry A. Dolan and Luisa Kroll, "Inside the 2014 Forbes Billionaires List: Facts and Figures," *Forbes*, March 3, 2014, and Katie Sola, "The 25 Countries with the Most Billionaires," *Forbes*, March 9, 2016. Quoted in Meghan O'Sullivan, *Windfall: How the New Energy Abundance Upends Global Politics and Strengthens America's Power* (New York: Simon & Schuster, 2017), 189 and 409–10.

56. Boris Nemtsov and Vladimir Milov asserted in 2011 that Gazprom's cost of construction would have been $3 million per km, two to three times higher than the world average. Andrei Shleifer and Daniel Treisman, "Why Moscow Says No," *Foreign Affairs,* January/February 2011: 127. EU sanctions, enacted in the aftermath of Russia's occupation of Crimea, made it much more difficult for Gazprom to raise money for the project and would have increased construction costs still further. Darya Korsunskaya, "Putin drops South Stream gas pipeline to Europe, courts Turkey," Reuters, December 1, 2014.

57. Natural gas from Central Asia has been described as a "core element in Gazprom's resource base." "Profiles: Alexey Miller/Gazprom," *European CEO*, August 4, 2014.

58. Uzbekistan is among the world's top ten producers of gold; Kyrgyzstan and Tajikistan likewise produce it. Azerbaijan produces some of the world's finest caviar.

59. This is why the political and economic arrangements through which power is exercised in the Russian Federation have been characterized as "crony capitalism."

60. Nearly all Western observers question the depth and sincerity of Putin's commitment to state sovereignty in the aftermath of Russia's invasion, occupation and annexation of Crimea and armed support for separatist forces in Ukraine. However, as we noted above, Putin sees Russia's actions in Crimea as a necessary defensive move to protect vital strategic assets, and its intervention in eastern Ukraine as undertaken taken in support of forces loyal to Ukraine's legitimate government and in fulfillment of Russia's treaty obligations.

61. Russia has therefore been helping China expand and strengthen its navy and participating in joint naval maneuvers in the South and East China Seas. Michael Paul, "Partnership on the High Seas: China's and Russia's Joint Naval Maneuvers," *Stiftung, Wissenschaft und Politik*, quoted in *Russia Matters*, May 29–June 3, 2019.

62. China has not endorsed Putin's moves in Crimea, but it has carefully refrained from criticizing them. In two UN Security Council votes on resolutions condemning his actions in March 2014, China abstained. Zhang Lihua, "Explaining China's Position on the Crimea Referendum," Carnegie-Tsinghua Center for Global Policy," April 1, 2015.

63. Camilla T.N. Sorenson and Ekaterina Klimenko, "Emerging Chinese-Russian Cooperation in the Arctic," Policy Paper 46, Stockholm International Peace Research Institute, June 2017.

64. Henry Foy, "Why China's Investment Play into Russia May Endure," *Financial Times*, September 12, 2018.

65. Holly Ellyatt, "Business leaders hail Russia's booming energy ties with China," CNBC, November 29, 2018.

66. Like their counterparts in Russia, Chinese officials are increasingly concerned about the growing possibility of terrorists coming out of Afghanistan. They have watched with alarm the recent rise of ISIS in that country. Just as the Russians worry about members of their Muslim population who have fought in Syria and Iraq and are now returning, the Chinese fear that Uighurs who joined jihadist organizations there will re-enter their country from Tajikistan. They are eager to cooperate with Russia to combat this threat under the aegis of the Counter-Terrorism Cooperation Center of the Shanghai Cooperation Organization. Mathieu Duchatel, "Terror Overseas: Understanding China's Evolving Counter-Terror Strategy," Policy Brief, European Council on Foreign Relations, October 2016.

67. "Central Asia's Economic Evolution From Russia to China," *Stratfor*, April 5, 2018.

68. Alexander Cooley, "Cooperation Gets Shanghaied," *Foreign Affairs*, December 14, 2009.

69. China's President Xi Jinping first broached the idea of Russia's participation in the BRI in 2013. Putin rejected the idea for six years. The Russian section of China's Meridian Toll Highway is now scheduled for completion in 2024. It has been suggested that Putin was ultimately forced to agree to the project as the price for obtaining additional Chinese investment in the Arctic and Siberia. "Putin Demands Role in Eurasian Part of Belt and Road," VOA, May 4, 2019.

70. Joshua Kucera, "China Building a Military Base on Afghan-Tajik Border," *Eurasianet*, January 7, 2018.

71. This has reportedly occurred in Myanmar, Pakistan, and Sri Lanka. Xue Gong, "Will China Undermine Its Own Influence in Southeast Asia Through the Belt and Road?" *The Diplomat*, April 13, 2019.

72. Richard D. Fisher, Jr., "China Militarizes Its Influence in Africa," *The National Interest*, November 25, 2018.

Chapter Two

Russia's Economic Weakness

Although the Russian Federation is still an "upper income" country accord-ing to ratings of the World Bank, its relative economic condition has deteri-orated since the breakup of the USSR. Russia's aggregate growth rate over the years 1990–2018 has been estimated at less than one percent per year, while the rest of the world was growing at about 2.5 percent. China grew much faster. Even "high income" countries grew at about 2 percent.[1] For a leader seeking to restore his country's great power status, this lackluster performance has served as a significant constraint. To understand Russia's relative weakness, we present a comprehensive socio-economic audit of its economy in three parts: current income and spending, a capital asset balance sheet, and long-term prospects.

ECONOMIC PERFORMANCE IN THE PUTIN ERA

During the first ten years of Putin's leadership, the Russian economy recov-ered from its historic decline of the 1990s and experienced a good 6 percent average yearly growth in its GDP. It last achieved the excellent growth rate of 8 percent in 2008. This was a period of rising commodity prices, higher revenues from exports, fewer distorting subsidies, near elimination of barter transactions, and a takeover of big businesses by ambitious young entrepren-eurs.[2] Russia was able to increase its oil production, reduce its gross debt, increase foreign direct investment considerably, raise wages several times over, and cut unemployment from 10.6 percent in 2000 to 6.2 percent in

2005–2008. The global financial crisis of 2008 and the oil price collapse ended this very favorable period.

After that, the economy slowed even through a short burst in the oil price. When volatile global oil prices dropped sharply in late 2014 to around $50 per barrel, Russia's GDP growth fell off drastically. The oil price collapse of 2014–2015 represented income loss of about $89 billion out of Russian exports of crude and refined oil—about a third of the total revenue from this source. Natural gas price cuts added a further loss of $35.9 billion. [3]

With unused capacity exhausted, Russia experienced no growth from 2014 to 2016. Since then its economy has recovered somewhat but growth has remained between 1 and 2 percent yearly, even with better energy prices. Sanctions resulting from the takeover of Crimea and the decline in trade with Ukraine have apparently lowered GDP growth by 1.5 percentage points. [4] Some of the remaining growth has come from increased arms production and some import substitution, according to the Bank of Russia, not new civilian production. Although the depressions of 2008 and 2014 were effectively countered by fiscal support from reserve funds, no basic reforms were undertaken. State-owned firms and banks, many of them headed by Putin's cronies, were the principal beneficiaries.

THE CURRENT ECONOMIC SITUATION

This decade-long deceleration of GDP from 2008–2019 (an estimated 1.5 percentage points over this period) has come in large part because Russia continues to rely for most of its hard-currency earnings on oil and gas. [5] The country produces about 11 million barrels a day (or 580 million tons a year), about the same as Saudi Arabia or the USA.

National Income

Global prices have recently recovered to about $60 barrel [6] because of reduced supplies from Venezuela, Iran, Libya, and elsewhere, giving Putin's regime some respite. In early 2019 Russia has a sizable current account surplus of 6.5 percent of its GDP, allowing a positive budgetary balance of 2.4 percent. [7] Still, because world *short-term* demand for oil and gas is inelastic, relatively small, unexpected changes in supply can raise (or reduce) the world price by a large amount. Understanding this fact, Russia has promised to join some members of the oil cartel (OPEC) to regulate output to replace output lost to Iranian sanctions and thus to stabilize the oil price. This would supposedly maintain long-term global demand, which is projected to increase by 1–2 percent yearly.[8] But the Russian share of the market appears to be capped, because internal financing of new discoveries to replace depletion within the Russian Federation is hardly possible without foreign participation.[9]

We believe increases or even maintenance of the oil and gas price will be temporary and insufficient to revive the Russian economy without major improvements in other sectors. Most petroleum experts believe, as we do, that prices will eventually return to the long-term cost of production of about $40, unless OPEC suppliers restrict output artificially (and unsustainably).[10] This is a major consequence of rising output in the U.S. Permian Basin. Technological advances in shale-oil (horizontal drilling) production have made the United States and other parts of the world nearly self-sufficient in liquid fuels. As evidence of their long range price forecasts, foreign oil companies have everywhere been abandoning previous plans for oil or gas exploitation. Solar, wind, and tidal methods have become as inexpensive as the more polluting coal and oil-fired electricity.[11] Investments in these renewable sources of electrical energy have increased, encouraged by private and public worries about climate deterioration. More efficient and less polluting electrical vehicles and other devices (such as air conditioning) are also forthcoming.

Aware of these prospects, President Putin (and Prime Minister Medvedev) has called for more diversification—but without effective action. When oil prices recover, as they did in 2009 and 2018, Putin has been reluctant to change. Frustrated at such inaction, long-time Finance Minister Alexei Kudrin resigned in 2011. Invited back in 2016, Kudrin was commissioned to formulate yet another plan to transform the Russian economy. He has suggested higher taxes and retirement ages, as well as police reform. These conservative reforms will be difficult to implement in Putin's Russia, as shown by demonstrative opposition to pension reform led by Alexei Navalny and others. A better climate for small, decentralized manufacturing, including bank credit, would be essential, too.

Besides the reduced energy receipts, a second negative effect on national income has come from the fall off of foreign investments. During the boom years of 2000–2014 a number of globally prominent companies invested in Russia.[12] Foreign firms might be still interested in the Russian market, as they were before 2014, if sanctions were lifted. But that will not necessarily happen. For instance, despite its persistent attempt, Walmart declined to enter the Russian market by purchasing one of the country's backward retail chains. A source familiar with this failure gave the reason: bureaucrats "did not want another whiner like Ikea, which had exposed corruption."[13] According to a survey in *The Moscow Times*, 62 percent of respondents say that normal business requires "deception." The "shadow economy" of illicit business is estimated there at 20 percent of all transactions.[14] That is a major deterrent to foreign investors.

Due to Western sanctions since 2014, credits to Russian energy, defense, and banking operations have been restricted by the United States and the EU. Foreign direct investments (FDI) in 2015 were only about 10 percent of the amounts in 2013. Compared to the previous year, FDI fell by half in 2018, according to Natalia Orlova of Alfa-Bank, the largest private bank in the country.[15] Because of this reduced flow of funds, the value of Russian securities and the ruble have fallen since 2014. The floating ruble remains substantially undervalued (64 per USD in mid-2019), making imports (and repayment of dollar debts) expensive.[16]

Government Expenditures

Despite budgetary surpluses (now about $41 billion) and a positive balance of payments, spending on popular civilian needs has been limited in favor of saving and defense outlays. In 2016 federal spending on education and health was slashed to less than 8 percent of the budget, while "law and order" and "defense" took more than one-third.[17] Very little infrastructure has been built, mostly around Moscow. The well-being of ordinary Russians has been sacrificed to meet the state's demands. According to Henry Foy, the Moscow bureau chief of the *Financial Times*, "Tepid growth, five years of falling incomes, high inflation, rising taxes and cuts to social handouts squeeze [Russia's] population."[18]

Although civilian needs have been largely ignored, total government spending under Putin has risen considerably with a $700 billion program for military modernization over a decade begun in 2010. Because of increased dependence on Russia's defense sector to replace imports, this costly part of the budget has ballooned.[19] It seems that civilian businesses are also being pressed to satisfy defense orders.[20] Ever since Soviet times, the well-provisioned defense sector also produces goods for the civilian market, such as baby carriages.[21] With some 20 percent of the world market, Russian arms have been an important export (often provided on credit), especially since

2014. There has been an increased sales effort since 2013 to sell arms to Egypt, Indonesia, and others, according to SIPRI.[22] Emphasis in the defense budget proper has been on special forces and air transport, rather than cheaper land forces. Though active troop (*Voisky*) levels have been reduced from those of a decade ago, salaries have been raised. Furthermore, according to former U.S. Secretary of Defense James Mattis, Russia has increased the number and variety of its nuclear weapons, an expensive decision. According to NATO's Joint Force Command, Russia is also investing "heavily" in submarines.[23] In sum, Russia spent some 3.8 percent or more of its GDP ($47 billion), on defense in 2017.[24] This percentage exceeds every other country in the world, except Saudi Arabia.

Budgetary Balance

What does Russia's slow growth mean for government finances now and in the future? Taxes on the two main energy exports of oil and natural gas provide about 40 percent of Russia's budget revenues. So reduced earnings on export earnings from these sources has meant restraint had to be imposed on domestic services and even some wage payments. President Putin, who remembers the wild inflation of the 1990s, has insisted on macroeconomic stability as a prime duty of government.[25] So have his appointees.[26] Lest inflation accelerate, budget deficits (once 8–9 percent of GDP during the world financial depression) had to be reduced from 3.7 percent to 1.5 percent in 2016–2017. In 2018 there was a 2.4 percent surplus—very unusual for a large country. Gross domestic saving is an amazing 27 percent of GDP. As a result of this conservative macroeconomic management by the Central Bank of Russia, consumer prices had risen only 5 percent yearly by 2019. With an interest rate of 8.2 percent on government bonds, that means savers earn least 3 percent *real* interest.[27] This fiscal "defensiveness"[28] was successful in retaining a credit rating of BB+ and even moderating the fall of the ruble's value and of the Russian stock market.[29] Early in 2019 large bonds were sold on the European market as a possible defense against additional sanctions.[30]

To add to the defensive fiscal posture, the Duma (dominated by Putin's United Russia party) decided, after much discussion, to raise the value-added tax (VAT) from 18 to 20 percent in 2019. This will add some $9–10 billion to state revenues. Raising the pensionable retirement ages to sixty-three for women and sixty-five for men will also reduce deficit spending. Because older Russians are supported almost entirely by pensions, this was very unpopular. Apparently some pension accumulations were confiscated to use in the Crimea and Ukraine.[31] The tax on pension accumulations (22 percent) may even have to be raised.[32]

Indeed, the short-term fiscal management by the Putin government has been impressive. Even so, as Timothy Ash of BlueBay Asset Management commented, "What is the point of having a good balance sheet if your economy is not growing?" Entrepreneurs are wary, knowing that they prosper only at the regime's pleasure. "Do you ever really own anything in Russia?" comments Ash.[33]

GOVERNMENT RESOURCES

As a result of budget savings liquid reserves available to the Putin government by mid-2018 had risen to $456 billion in foreign currencies with an increased portion in gold.[34] Net of the modest foreign debt,[35] these financial reserves are obviously important to sustain an ambitious foreign policy, which involves uncertain costs. As a result of sanctions imposing penalties on Western banks which issue loans to large government-owned enterprises in Russia, this source of funds has been very substantially reduced.[36] Moreover, despite their existing Russian government debt holdings at high interest rates, foreign lenders have been increasingly reluctant to purchase more such debt because they "have little confidence in [Russia's] future."[37]

If Westerners are barred from or reluctant to invest in Russia, exceptional financial support could come from China, which has already contributed to the government's liquid resources. Between 2000 and 2014 Chinese official sources provided $36.6 billion in loans and grants, according to an AidData study.[38] Most of this went to public companies, Rosneft (14 percent share) and Transneft as loans, with the remainder of the flow to various Russian banks. Russian-owned Caspian Investment Resources, one of Russia's largest investors in Caspian Sea oil, was sold to Sinopec, the Chinese half-partner, for $1.2 billion.[39] In 2015 Gazprom sold 20 percent of its shares in Sila Sibiri, a major natural gas pipeline in Eastern Siberia, to China's Silk Road Fund. The People's Republic is now cooperating with Russia on some new projects in transportation—for example, a fast train from Moscow to Kazan. The two governments share joint ownership of a railroad and copper processing plant located in Mongolia. One sign of the Russian government's financial needs has been its willingness to permit Chinese investments and cooperation in Arctic ventures, such as explorations for gas on the Yamal Peninsula. While most of China's announced Belt and Road Initiative (BRI) investments are elsewhere, if Russia would need a loan with few questions asked, China is a possible source. The extent of Russia's pragmatic partnership with China is considered further in Chapter 7.

Another possible source of new money would be the Persian Gulf. Late in 2018 the non-aligned, but wealthy and ambitious, emirate of Qatar purchased 19.5 percent of Rosneft for $11.37 billion. If loans are insufficient, a less convenient way to raise cash would be to sell state property, such as Aeroflot, Sovkomflot, or Moscow real estate. Putin has been reluctant to do this, as their prices have fallen on the stock market since 2014 and have not yet fully recovered.[40] Obviously in a time of global tension, such sales would be difficult.

PUBLIC REACTIONS

Current government budget allocations, which do strengthen state power, do not escape public opinion. Sanctions and the weaker ruble caused by spending abroad by Putin's cronies have meant higher prices and lower availability of what the average Russian buys. When Putin imposed counter-sanctions banning agricultural imports from the EU, higher quality fruits and vegetables became more expensive. Ordinary Russian citizens faced declining real incomes in 2016–2018 and were worried about worse declines in the future, according to surveys by the Levada Center, an independent polling organization in Russia. Vodka and caviar were out of reach for most, even for special occasions. Most Russians are "compliant" with government actions but feel "the Kremlin is paying too much attention to foreign policy and neglects domestic problems."[41] Increases in official retirement ages are being blamed for weaker-than-expected showings for the ruling United Russia party in recent regional elections.[42] Four of the Kremlin's candidates for governor outside Moscow were defeated, a previously unknown failure.[43] Putin's own popularity has fallen from 80–90 percent to 48 percent, with retirement- age seniors (who had been strong supporters of Putin), young people, and the poor (once his main support) indicating less trust in the president. Indeed, Putin once said "Pension guarantees are probably the biggest achievement and the biggest problem for our country."[44] Public opinion cannot be ignored, even when votes can be manipulated.

LONG-TERM PROSPECTS

Russia's long-term capability to maintain world power and influence, including influence in the Near Abroad, depends on more than armaments and cash in government coffers. A modern conventional and nuclear arsenal is obviously necessary to deter aggression against Russia by other major powers and repel any assault that might occur. The government can exert influence by using the cash at its disposal to bribe or invest in other countries. However, Russia's economic strength is also a crucial determinant of its relative power. Any assessment of that power must therefore take into account key factors that affect its economic strength today and will continue to do so in the future. These include the size and composition of the population in general and the labor force in particular, the amount of corruption plaguing the economy and society, and overall economic structure.

Population and Labor Trends

As a result of poor health and out-migration, Russia's population since 1990 shrank from 146.9 million to 142.2.[45] Some 8 million Russians are heroin-like users, and HIV/AIDS infections are growing without any effective treatments available to many.[46] An estimated 56,730 people emigrated from the Russian Federation in 2016, four times the rate in 2011.[47] About 2.7 million Russian-born citizens, many with higher education, already live outside Russia.[48] According to a survey of Russian expatriates in four U.S. cities, this brain-drain accelerated after the slowdown of 2013.[49] Somewhat offsetting these losses are migrants from troubled Ukraine and Muslim areas of Russia's south.[50]

Life expectancy among Russians as estimated by the World Health Organization is only 70.5 years, compared to 78–82 for developed Western countries. This reflects (male) morbidity from alcoholism. The crude birth rate as of 2008 was 12 per thousand against its high death rate of 15 per thousand.[51] Currently, therefore, the Russian Federation's population is not growing at all.[52] Many experts predict that it will continue to decline. By 2030, according to a UN projection, the population will be between 122 and 135 million, as compared with 146.8 now, including 2.3 million from Crimea. The working age population will fall, too, more than 10 percent from the 104 million now. By 2030, according to one demographer, each pensioner will be supported by only one worker, leading to a declining growth rate, even to zero, according to one observer.[53]

A labor shortage could be relieved by facilitating movement of under-employed labor from stagnant areas to those needing workers. Such movement is unusual in Russia, however, because politicians discourage layoffs for fear of discontent and also because of the shortage of affordable housing in the few dynamic areas (especially Moscow and St. Petersburg). The housing shortage there would require massive investments to rectify.

Quite obviously, economic prosperity depends on active-age citizens. But Russia's future prospects are not encouraging in the eyes of its young and technically educated population. The unemployment rate has been as high as 8.2 percent, though it has tapered off to 4.7 percent as of early 2019. Some young people have found employment in the military, law and finance, construction, aerospace, or in Russia's IT and cyber-warfare efforts, but many with more peaceful ambitions have left for the West, like some of the Russian super-rich. According to a poll by the highly respected Levada Center, 22 percent of Russia's adult population would like to leave the country for good—more than the number several years ago. That includes even higher fractions of younger, high-income adults. One expatriate, Google co-founder Sergey Brin, has described his native land as "Nigeria with snow." Reflecting a similar attitude, 77 percent of Russian science and engineering students studying in America replied that they will not go back to their native land.[54] Among entrepreneurs and students, more than half would leave permanently, and about a third of professionals would like to do so.[55] The leading causes mentioned were "an unreasonably high cost of living, low quality of medical services, and widespread corruption among public servants."

Corruption

Corruption has a major impact on the strength of the economy (and government resources) because it unnecessarily inflates the cost of anything the government purchases or builds. It also has significant implications for popular morale and thus regime stability, another requirement of great power status. One highly visible form of corruption occurs in road building, a project emphasized by Putin in his effort to improve Russia's aging infrastructure. According to one estimate, roads in the Russian Federation cost 38 times more than those built in Canada, a country with similar topography and climate.[56] According to a report in 2015, of state purchases 95 percent are uncompetitive and 40 percent are made from a single supplier. Clearly, this allows corruption. Another poll by Levada during the summer of 2017 found that one-third of Russians questioned replied that corruption has "fully permeated the country's government from top to bottom." According to one estimate, the top 3 percent of the population own 89 percent of the country's assets.[57] An income distribution of this sort is often associated with corruption. An estimated 42 percent of Levada's respondents felt that President Putin is "in large part responsible for this."[58]

Corruption also leads to an outflow of much needed capital. Campden Media and UBS asked nineteen Russian businessmen with more than $50 million in personal assets about their plans. Of these seventeen said they had moved their wealth abroad and might sell their companies, whose turnover exceeded $100 million, rather than passing them on to their children. (These offspring are now typically studying in the West for future business careers there.[59]) According to a recent source, Russian millionaires keep more than two-thirds of their wealth outside the country's banks.[60] To safeguard illicit gains, some considerable capital has flowed outwards to London, Cyprus, or elsewhere.[61] Nadia Wells of the global fund Capital Group commented "if your elite is not reinvesting in Russia, why should we invest here?" She noted that compared with other emerging markets Russian assets—such as energy fields—trade at a discount of as much as 40 percent.[62] Foreign firms might be interested in the Russian market, as they were before 2014, if sanctions were lifted. But ever-growing corruption might dissuade them.

The prospects are poor that this will change. In 2017 Russia ranked 135 among the least corrupt countries in the world. Putin has declared his determination to curb corruption, but his power is heavily dependent on it. Moreover, there appears to be close connection between corruption and the rule of law, and that is another area in which Russia is extremely weak.[63]

Economic Structure

The longer term, post-Putin prospects for the Russian economy will not improve without a major change in economic structure. Finance Minister A.G. Siluanov has stated that "the state is enforcing a new style of management. It will come from the top and go to the bottom."[64] This is doubling down on a failing model, in our opinion. Oil and gas production volumes are stable worldwide, while competition from LNG (liquefied natural gas) from Qatar and other producers and shale oil/gas from North America are cutting into the Russian share.[65] Without new discoveries, depletion and deterioration of Russian wells can be expected. Prices of oil and natural gas have fluctuated wildly and cannot be relied on, as we argued above. Because of technological advances, oil and gas will eventually be replaced as sources of electric power by renewables—photo-voltaic cells, large capacity batteries and hydro storage to provide power when the wind or sun is not available. BP, the energy firm that reports on world energy trends, expects that these renewables will account for half of the global energy supply growth over the next twenty years.

Though once prone to brag about his country as an "energy superpower," President Putin knows the country must do better—and differently. But he simply reinforces reliance on state-run entities.[66] Industrial and R&D investments have been paltry.[67] Many sectors, according to an official survey, have obsolete equipment.[68] Russia has too few new small and medium enterprises, which are often sources of new ideas. Foreign investors with no political support are sometimes pushed out, according to Kudrin. Little has been done to increase productive investments. Despite a high *gross* savings rate, the basic problem has been the failure to invest in new domestic capacity. Since the fall of the Soviet Union only one cement factory has been built and no new oil refinery. A World Bank study from 2007 found that only five percent of firms were renewed in the previous decade—a quarter of the rate in healthy Western economies. Russia's state banks, which would have to finance new investments, control some 60 percent of the country's assets.[69] According to banker Natalia Orlova, most of the investments in 2017 were for three large state-backed, prestige projects, including the renovation of Moscow, the new bridge to Crimea, and a gas pipeline to China. The foreign investment available for new industries and products is less than it was before 2014. Investment is now less attractive because of the mounting control by the security services and Putin himself. To fund the bridge to Crimea a huge investment of $3.7 billion was provided to Arkady Rotenberg, Putin's childhood judo partner and one of his closest collaborators, although ferry service could have been expanded at a small fraction of the cost.[70] For the last decade or so, the Putin regime has centralized much of the economy in the hands of his trusted associates an arrangement called "crony capitalism." These men run "entire industries."[71] In 2005 state ownership was 35 percent of the economy; it is now 70 percent, according to the Federal Anti-Monopoly Service.[72]

Making deals with intimates probably favors Moscow where, according to the World Bank's *Ease of Doing Business,* commercial conditions have improved, but not necessarily elsewhere.[73] Tech firms there, such as Yandex and VKontakte, successfully compete with Google and Facebook, showing the availability of talent. The country's Gini coefficient of 41.5 in 2015 shows relatively high inequality with Moscow and St. Petersburg leading all the other provinces. This, of course, reduces the likelihood of competition, a major incentive. [74] One exception has been Rostelmash, the agricultural machinery producer in Rostov (far from Moscow), which exports to thirty-five countries.

The main problems for Russia's long-term future are thus structural and institutional. Population and labor trends are unfavorable and corruption appears to be endemic. Productivity is unlikely to increase without major reform of economic structure. However, the experience of devastating decline in the 1990s has soured most Russians with regard to economic reform. The prospects for it are poor. Yet neither military modernization nor new pipelines have improved the prospects of renewed economic growth.

RELATIVE ECONOMIC POWER

Russia's ability to influence others must be judged comparatively. Although its relative overall material strength has declined relative to other major powers, its military spending has been sustained, growing perhaps to over 5 percent of GDP in its stagnant overall economy. However, the United States has been spending about 3.6 percent of its much larger GDP, [75] and its chief NATO allies add perhaps $200 billion to the American $609 billion. Clearly Russia and its allies in the Near Abroad (which spend very little on defense) are at a vast material disadvantage.

As we demonstrate in Chapter 4, Russia is losing the financial ability to extend its foreign activities and investments in the Near Abroad. By contrast, China has been growing at rates of 6–9 percent. Its defense spending of $145 billion (less than 2 percent of its GDP) exceeds Russia's by around $100 billion. As of 2016 China's total trade was greater than Russia's, especially on the export side. [76] China is now joining with a Russian shipping firm to send goods and LNG to Europe in ice breaking ships over the Arctic route. [77]

In short, if Putin's ambitions and policies had not been tailored to the means Russia can command from its unreformed economy dependent on its oil, gas, and other natural resources, together with loans it can exact from China, his country would appear less powerful. Russia's military strength, which remains formidable, is an important component of its power, and Putin has used it successfully to ensure Russia's dominance of the Near Abroad and deter further attempts to encroach on its self-proclaimed "sphere of privileged interest." However, the costs of relying on force are notable, as demonstrated by the sanctions from which Russia has suffered considerably since 2014, along with the diplomatic isolation that has accompanied them. Russia's limited economic means have thus constrained Putin's ability to pursue great power status, which is difficult to achieve by military instruments alone. That constraint is likely to remain when Putin is no longer in charge.

NOTES

1. *World Development Indicators 2016* and CIA *Factbook*, accessed 2018. Thus Russia fell behind "high income" countries, including the United States and EU, by about 20 percent.

2. For example, Roman Abramovich at Sibneft (an oil company), Oleg Deripaska at Rusal (aluminum), and Sergei Popov at SUEK (coal).

3. Atlas@mit.edu, using World Bank figures.

4. These are considered "credible figures," to which should be added the impact of counter-sanctions and loss of foreign direct investment, making a total loss of 1.5 percentage points. *Kommersant* Deputy Editor- in-Chief Dmitry Butrin, March 12, 2019. *Current Digest of the Russian Press* [CD] 71, no. 11: 4.

5. *Russia Matters*, accessed September 2018.

6. This is the international Brent standard; the New York price is about $6 less per barrel.

7. *The Economist,* April 27, 2019, p. 76.

8. Christopher Alessi, "OPEC, Russia Hike Oil Output as Iran Production Falters," *Wall Street Journal*, October 11, 2018. This increase would probably come from India and other developing countries.

9. Mikhail Krutikin, *Slon.ru*, August 11, 2015. CD 67, no. 33: 18.

10. Predictions of the future oil price vary strikingly: the International Energy Agency predicts a $60 oil price by 2060, but Oil Change International says $35. In 2016 the oil price reached $26 per barrel. According to Russian Finance Minister Anton Siluanov, with present tax rates, budget balance would require an oil price of only $40/barrel. But this does not allow for any increases in defense, pension or healthcare spending.

11. Technological change will mean falling costs of alternative methods of producing liquid fuels or electricity. The *Economist*, August 11, 2018.

12. These included IKEA, Auchan of France, and Metro from Germany. Among the investors in the relatively well-governed Kaluga region were Volkswagen, Volvo, L'Oreal, AstraZeneca. Chris Miller, *Putinomics: Power and Money in Resurgent Russia* (Chapel Hill, NC: University of North Carolina, 2018), 87–93. With real wages growing rapidly before 2014, the modern supermarket chain Magnit was able to expand more broadly, too.

13. Miller, *Putinomics*, 87-93.

14. Cited in *Russia Matters,* February 22, 2019.

15. *The Economist,* September 1, 2018. The total for 2018 was only $88 billion, much less than previously.

16. This 2018 valuation by is based on the *The Economist's* famous "Big Mac" index, which shows 57 percent undervaluation as against the U.S. dollar. The ruble fell by 13.9 percent against the dollar from the spring of 2018 to February 2019. *The Economist,* February, 23, 2019.

17. Ministry of Finance, quoted in Miller, *Putinomics*, p. 106.

18. Quoted in *Russia Matters*, accessed April 15, 2019. Consumer prices have been rising about 5 percent yearly. Inflation-adjusted discretionary incomes have fallen more than 13 percent over the last nine years.

19. M. Bodner, "Putin Urges Rapid Switch to Domestic Production in Defense Industry," *The Moscow Times*, July 28, 2014.

20. Evidence for this was a recent State Duma proposal to institute criminal liability for any business owner who refuses to implement state defense orders. Aleksandr Golts, *The New York Times*, Nov. 23, 2017. CD 69, no. 47: 13.

21. Owing to different quality-control needs, military and civilian production lines are still often separate.

22. *The Economist*, August 18, 2018, 52.

23. *Russia Matters*, October 15, 2018.

24. *World Almanac 2018*, 826. The CIA *Factbook* gives a 5.4 percent figure for military expenditures in 2017. The probable existence of secret items and the lack of figures for border troops, pensions, and other defense-related spending make these figures inexact. *Russia Matters* staff estimates showed reduced defense spending in 2016–2017 and a 2018 planned increase from 2.84 to 2.95 trillion rubles (August 22, 2018). Since defense spending is mostly domestic, efforts to translate these artificial bookkeeping amounts to the U.S. dollar are liable to mislead. Another estimate (quoted in IISS, February 18, 2017, 73), based on the UN methodology, indicated that outlays on the military amounted to 5.7 percent of GDP in 2016. However, about 21 percent of defense spending is "classified," and not included (Ivan Tkachov and Anton Feinberg, *RBC Daily*, August 30, 2017). According to Michael Kofman of CNA International, total Russian defense spending has been $150–180 billion, figured at purchasing power parity, which would make it 31–37 percent of the GDP of $481 billion. *Russia Matters*, May 6, 2019.

25. Speech to the Federal Assembly, September 4, 2004.

26. Recent chairs of the Central Bank of Russia, Sergei Ignatiev (2000–2013) and Elvira Nabiullina (2013–present), both competent professionals close to Putin, have been described as "systemic liberals," that is, "liberals who work within the system." Anders Åslund, *Russia's Crony Capitalism: The Path from Market Economy to Kleptocracy* (New Haven, CT: Yale University Press), 72.

27. *The Economist*, April 6, 2019, 76.

28. With both government and bank rates about 10 percent, the *real* rate of interest on loans to private businesses is about 5 percent.

29. *The Economist*, June 2, 2018, 80.

30. Max Seddon and Nikou Asgari, "Russia ramps up bond sales ahead of possible U.S. sanctions," *Financial Times*, May 8, 2019.

31. According to Finance Minister Anton Siluanov, quoted in Leonard Bershidsky, "Russian Pensions Paid for Putin's Crimea Grab," *Bloomberg*, June 20, 2014.

32. Andrey Movchan of the Carnegie Moscow Center, *Russia Matters*, October 10, 2018.

33. *The Economist*, March 1, 2018. Apparently this economic defensiveness is "to help Russia weather future sanctions and build defenses against the West," according to Ash.

34. CD 70, no. 30: 9–10. This appears to be enough to cover the official foreign debt of $540 million, which had been much higher four years earlier. The foreign personal household, non-financial corporate, and government debt payable in foreign currencies is 25 percent of GDP, less than Poland's (51 percent).

35. Russia's foreign debt in 2018 was 27.4 percent of its nominal GDP in dollars. www.CEICdata.com/en/country/russia. (July 14, 2019).

36. The Russian government owns, partly or wholly, more than 500,000 enterprises. Alexander Abramov, Alexander Radygin and Maria Chernova, "State-owned enterprises in the Russian market: Ownership structure and their role in the economy," *Russian Journal of Economics* 3:1 (2017). Since 2014, sanctions have been directed at some of the largest of these, including Russia's major banks, energy companies, arms producers, and transportation and construction firms. *Radio Free Europe/Radio Liberty*, September 19, 2018.

37. *Inside Russia*, Carnegie Foundation for International Peace, May 25, 2016, quoting Chris Miller of Yale University.

38. Published by the College of William and Mary AidData research lab. This was the highest total to any country. Bethany A. Abrahmian, "Russia Is the Biggest Recipient of Chinese Foreign Aid," *Foreign Policy*, October 11, 2017.

39. Peter Leonard, "Economy and Sanctions Derail Russia's Central Asian Investments," *Eurasianet*, January 28, 2016.

40. As of March, 2017, the Russian stock market had fallen another 8 percent from the end of 2016 to 2017, but stabilized by April, 2019.

41. *The Economist*, May 12, 2018. According to Denis Volkov of the Levada Center, Russians "may consider their country's greatness on the international stage to be Putin's main accomplishment, but the public is growing disillusioned with Russia's isolation, the unresolved conflict with the West, and the fact that the country is constantly 'helping others' at the expense of its own citizens." *The Economist*, December 1, 2018.

42. "Russians Split in Attitudes to Ruling United Russia Party," *The Moscow Times,* September 12, 2018.

43. "Putin Continues Governor Reshuffle after Election Snag," *The Moscow Times*, October 2, 2018.

44. Chris Miller, 107. According to Miller, part of the Kremlin's strategy for maintaining power has been to prevent popular discontent by guaranteeing low unemployment and adequate pensions.

45. The main problem is the shortfall of births during the depressed 1990s. Irina Denisova and Judith Shapiro, "Recent Demographic Developments in the Russian Federation," Michael Alexeev and Shlomo Weber, *The Oxford Handbook of the Russian* Economy (New York: Oxford University Press, 2013), 800–25. The World Bank gives a higher figure of 144.4 million in 2017, still below the 1990 number.

46. Laruelle, M. and Radvanyi, J. *Understanding Russia* (Lanham: Rowman & Littlefield, 2018), 25.

47. Zhanna Nemtsova, "Young, Liberal and Russian," *The New York Times*, September 23, 2018. According to a recent Gallup poll, 20 percent of Russians would like to move; 44 percent among those ages fifteen to twenty-eight. *Russia Matters*, accessed April 5, 2019.

48. According to the Gaidar Economic Institute, *Russia Matters*, October 10, 2018.

49. John Herbst and Sergei Erofiev, "The Putin Exodus," *The Atlantic Council* Report, cited in *Russia Matters*, accessed February 25, 2019.

50. *World Almanac 2018*, 826. Total migration for 2012–2017 was 1.6 million, according to official sources. Of an estimated 8 percent migrants in the Russian population as a whole, some 400,000 are from Ukraine. Muslim migrants from the Caucasus area generally have less education than the Russian population and thus do little to compensate for the brain drain. *Russia Matters*, accessed November 2, 2018.

51. *World Development* Indicators 2010, 64. Total fertility of 1.7–1.8 can barely support natural increase, and it probably reflects the higher rates in the Muslim south.

52. *World Almanac 2018*, 826, gives a population growth of 0.1 percent.

53. Steve Johnson, "Russia's Potential Growth Rate 'Close to Zero,'" *Financial Times,* April 13, 2016.

54. *The Economist*, September 10, 2011, 30.

55. *The Economist*, September 10, 2011, 27. This was a World Bank survey. To leave permanently means obtaining entry visas, contracts, or student fellowships—not easy matters.

56. Victoriia Nikitina, *Argumenty i Fakty,* June 8, 2011, cited in Laruelle and Radvanyi, 81.

57. "Richest 3 Percent Russians Hold 90 Percent of Country's Financial Assets," *The Moscow Times,* April 12, 2019.

58. Paul Richardson, "How Much Worse?" *Russian Life*, November/December, 2017, 4.

59. *The Economist*, September 10, 2011, 30.

60. "Russian Millionaires Hold Two-thirds of Their Money Abroad, Report Says," *The Moscow Times*, October 31, 2018.

61. Sergei Guriev,"Russia's Constrained Economy," *Foreign Affairs*, 95:3 (May–June, 2016): 18–22.

62. Gregory L. White, "Putin Touts Russian Economic Power," *The Wall Street Journal*, October 7, 2011.

63. Laruelle and Radvanyi, 90–91. The World Bank's index of "governmental effectiveness" rates rule of law, accountability, political stability, and lack of domestic violence. It has not improved much since 2008 and stands at 22 out of an ideal score of 100. Quoted in Andrew E. Kramer, "With Savings to Burn, Russia Turns (Again) to a State-Led Spending Plan," *The New York Times*, February 6, 2019.

64. Quoted in Kramer, "With Savings to Burn."

65. *The Economist,* February 26, 2017, 11. Poland is asking for cheaper gas and will use the line from Norway as an alternative source. Ukraine stopped buying the expensive Russian gas in 2015 and is buying from EU sources. It wants a 25 percent discount. "Russia says Ukraine decision to stop buying Russian gas is political," Reuters, June 30, 2015.

66. According to the Federal Anti-Monopoly Service, the state's share of the Russian GDP has now risen to 70 percent. *Russia Matters,* May 10, 2019.

67. In 2016 expenditures on R&D were 1.10 percent of GDP. By comparison, the figure for Israel was 4.25 percent, for Japan 3.14 percent, Germany 2.94 percent ,and the United States 2.74 percent. "Research and Development Expenditures (percent of GDP)," The World Bank Group, 2019.

68. Laruelle and Radvanyi, 73.

69. Bloomberg, quoted in *The Economist,* September 2, 2017, 64.

70. Radio Free Europe/Radio Liberty, May 15, 2018; Alec Luhn, "Putin Opens Bridge to Crimea," *The Telegraph*, May 15, 2018.

71. *Russia Matters,* accessed December 7, 2018.

72. According to Rosstat, the share of fixed assets in private or mixed-ownership companies in 2013 was 82 percent, but of course this can hide the role of oligarchs in their control. Cf. Laruelle and Radvanyi, 82. The neglected health and education sectors are privately managed, except for those reserved for the privileged, as are small shops.

73. This World Bank survey, which concentrated only on Moscow, rated Russia as 35th out of 190 countries in 2018, giving Russia favorable ratings on tax collection and enforcing contracts. N. Kudrin quoted in *Russia Matters*, December 7, 2018.

74. N. Kudrin quoted in *Russia Matters*, December 7, 2018.

75. Russia's GDP is about one-fifteenth that of the United States.

76. The EU is China's largest merchandise trade partner. www.ec.europa.edu (June 12, 2019).

77. Costas Paris, "China, Russia Carriers to Ship Gas on Arctic Route," *The Wall Street Journal*, June 11, 2019.

Chapter Three

Disappointing Multilateral Institutions

Ever since the dissolution of the USSR in 1991, Russian leaders have promoted a number of arrangements to retrieve and reinforce the influence Moscow once exerted on its neighbors in order to regain unquestioned great power status. To fortify a country's role as a major international power, pursuit of close associations with like-minded, historically subordinate states is a common strategy. France maintains financial and military relations with its former colonies in Africa and elsewhere; the British Commonwealth replaced its Empire after World War II. The United States maintains geostrategically significant relationships with its accessions dating from the Spanish-American War of 1898—such as Puerto Rico, Guam and for almost half a century, the Philippines (independent since 1946). As a permanent member of the UN Security Council from its inception, the Russian Federation would want to emulate these coequals, as had the USSR.

As we have noted in Chapter 1, moreover, President Putin has been highly influenced by the ideas of Evgeny Primakov, post-Soviet Russia's most distinguished Foreign Minister. Primakov believed that restoration of Russia's great power status would be greatly aided by the gradual emergence of a multi-polar international system in the post-Cold War world. In such a system, the power of the West in general and the United States in particular would be balanced by the power of many new, competing power centers. Russia should not passively await the development of this new world order. Rather, it should actively promote it by strengthening and forming new alliances, if possible, dominated by Russia. Each of these alliances would constitute a pole of power in this multi-polar world.

THE COMMONWEALTH OF INDEPENDENT STATES

Of the original fourteen Soviet Union republics besides the Russian Federation, nine agreed in 1992-3 to become members of a new entity, the Commonwealth of Independent States (CIS).[1] As of 2019 eight full members of the CIS remain besides Russia, plus associated Turkmenistan. Ukraine, never a full participant, has declared its intention to cease all cooperation with the organization. Georgia had been a CIS member from 1993 but withdrew in 2009. The headquarters of the CIS are located in Minsk, Belarus.

The states that agreed to join the CIS provided at least rhetorical support for Russia's foreign policy initiatives for the first decade and a half. But at an important meeting in 2008, some of the leaders had the effrontery to express disapproval of Russia's invasion of Georgia, a heretofore rare Russian use of force. Kazakhstan's then-president Nursultan Nazarbaev, one of Russia's best friends, released this statement just after the invasion: "The principle of territorial integrity is recognized by the entire international community. Difficult interethnic issues should be worked out through peaceful negotiations. There can be no military solution for such conflicts." In 2014 most of the other members disapproved of Russia's actions in the Crimea and eastern Ukraine or remained silent on the matter. Azerbaijan criticized the presence of Russian troops during the Crimean referendum on the future of the territory; Kyrgyzstan condemned "actions aimed at destabilizing the situation in Ukraine," and Belarus declared its support for maintaining Ukraine's territorial integrity.[2] President Nazarbaev added that Kazakhstan would collaborate with Ukraine's defense industry, an unusual slight to a powerful Russian industry. He also offered to send coal to Ukraine to offset shortages caused by pro-Russian rebels there. So much for rhetorical unity! Putin could not have been pleased.

CIS provisions also call for a free trade area throughout the region, but this ideal has lain dormant for years, although Russia does import goods from the rest of the members. Five of the CIS members now participate in a loosely applied customs union, now part of the Eurasian Economic Union (EaEU), discussed below. For about a decade Belarus and Ukraine received cheap gas from the pipelines which run through their territories. Indeed, for many years Belarus survived by importing cheap Siberian oil from Russia which it then refined to be sold in the West at a market price. This benefit was estimated at $50 billion over two decades.[3]

The effectiveness of the CIS as an instrument of Russian foreign economic policy has been limited ever since the Russian ruble lost its role as source of money and credit in 1993. Fewer than ten percent of the economic agreements signed in the CIS still exist—leaving only visa-free travel for Central Asians seeking employment in Russia.

Thus, CIS officials have little to do besides arranging more gatherings.[4] At one meeting of the organization, supposedly a coordinating body through which Russia tries to exercise leadership, only six of the presidents from member states bothered to show up. The meeting adjourned after thirty minutes. At the twentieth anniversary celebration of the CIS in Dushanbe, Tajikistan, three of the presidents again declined to attend. According to Alexei Malashenko of Moscow's liberal Carnegie Center, the countries of the former Soviet Union see such organizations as the CIS and EaEU, "as ruled by Russia, and they would like to deal with Russia in private."[5] Like the members of the European Union, when it comes to financial and tariff arrangements, CIS members wish to express their independence in different ways. Putin himself once conceded that the CIS was merely a form of "civilized divorce" for the states that had once constituted the USSR.[6]

THE COLLECTIVE SECURITY TREATY ORGANIZATION

To complement and strengthen the CIS in security matters, Russia induced five other members to join it in signing a Collective Security Treaty in 1992. Eager to give institutional shape to this alliance, Putin established the Collective Security Treaty Organization in 2002 and instituted yearly exercises involving members' troops.[7] One of the largest of these, conducted in Central Asia and Southern Russia in 2011, involved more than ten thousand troops and seventy combat aircraft. The timing and official comments suggest that the purpose in Putin's mind was to ensure that members were prepared to deal with domestic upheaval comparable that which had been underway in the Arab Spring.[8]

When this alliance was first formed, Russian President Boris President Yeltsin denied that it was meant to resemble NATO with its elaborate headquarters in Brussels and active missions.[9] In later years, however, President Putin began to depict the CSTO as a counterweight to NATO.[10] The resemblance is hard to see. Although in 2009 Putin instituted a Collective Rapid Reaction Force, which now has more than twenty-five thousand troops, these have never been used in action. This may be owing to the fact that the members have often disagreed on whether and when it should be deployed.[11] There is also a small "peace-keeping force" available for global conflicts, but Western countries have blocked UN endorsement of its use in conflict areas outside the CIS area; CSTO members have been unsupportive. Putin sought to use it to keep the peace in Eastern Ukraine, but the Security Council refused to approve such an operation and Russia's allies in the CSTO rejected the idea.[12] Putin has likewise been eager to use CSTO peacekeepers in Syria, but only Armenia has agreed, and no one has expected the Security Council to approve such a plan.[13]

High among Russia's security concerns has been defense of the external CIS borders from Islamists based in Afghanistan or supported by allies there. The forces of Kyrgyzstan, Tajikistan, Uzbekistan, and Turkmenistan, located on the east and south of the Russian Federation, are therefore consulted and trained with this in mind. However, military cooperation has been constrained by the unwillingness of the latter two states to participate in the CSTO. Some Russian units are stationed in southern Tajikistan, assisting Tajik forces in providing more robust protection along the border with Afghanistan. However, when Islamist rebels have been active in Tajikistan, Uzbekistan, and southern Kyrgyzstan, these threats have been dealt with unilaterally by the affected governments, not by CSTO units.[14] Uzbekistan's own forces put down the riotous uprising in Andijan in 2005 by themselves. Indeed, the Russian-dominated CSTO refused to become involved in clashes in the south of Kyrgyzstan between Uzbek and Kyrgyz communities in 2010, despite the request from the then Kyrgyz president Rosa Otunbaeva. Reportedly Uzbekistan objected to actions so close to its border, it is reported, so Russia backed away.[15]

Probably most disappointing to Putin is the small number of CIS states that have been willing to participate in the CSTO or have vacillated in this regard. During his long presidency, Uzbekistan's President Islam Karimov subscribed to the Collective Security Treaty in 1992 but withdrew in 1999. He was appreciative of Russia's verbal support for the brutal suppression of a riot in Andijan in 2005 and joined the CSTO the following year, but he left the alliance for the second time in 2012 after Russia began to insist that it must have the right to veto other members' ability to host foreign military bases on their soil. Some observers believe the Uzbek leader was hoping the United States would establish a military base in Afghanistan as it began withdrawing American troops from that country.[16] Both the EaEU and the CSTO, Karimov declared, reminded him too much of the Former Soviet

Union.[17] Even while Uzbekistan was a member, he refused to sign up for the Collective Rapid Reaction Force. Uzbekistan also strongly protested a plan to build a second Russian military base in the south of the Kyrgyz Republic near the Uzbek border. It never came about.[18] Moscow therefore proposed that a "reorganized" CSTO henceforth work by majority rule, not unanimity. As a result of these objections, the Russian head of the CSTO at the time, General Nikolai Bordyuzha, suggested that after consultations, the CSTO should express a joint position on international issues, as the EU and NATO occasionally do.[19] Nothing has been heard of this idea since.

No doubt the CSTO rubric assists its non-Russian members, though in ways which conform to Russian needs. It offers Russia's neighbors protection against threats from beyond the borders of the CIS: as in NATO, members promise to regard aggression against one as aggression against all. Under the CSTO aegis, Russian military academies offer training to Central Asian officers, as well as weapons and armaments of Russian manufacture at reduced rates.[20] The organization's military exercises address threats to all its members, especially those in Central Asia and the Caucasus. Its largest exercise, held in 2017, for example, simulated conflicts erupting in those two regions. With all member states participating, CSTO troops rehearsed a terrorist incursion into a member state. The portion involving a conventional adversary was staged in Armenia.[21] Thus the presumed opponent was probably Yerevan's longtime foe, Azerbaijan.

However, most Western observers think the CSTO exists primarily to further Russian policy goals rather than genuinely collective interests.[22] It has been moderately successful in that regard. Members pledge not to join other military alliances or groups of states, thereby limiting the possible inroads NATO might make into the Near Abroad. Russian air and land forces may make use of bases on the territory of CSTO member states from time to time, and Russia maintains its own bases in Kyrgyzstan, Tajikistan, and Armenia. As we have seen, Moscow has been granted the right to veto the establishment of new foreign military bases on the soil of other members. Russia's military cooperation with CSTO member states has intensified in the wake of the Ukraine crisis. Russia has signed new military deals with Belarus, Armenia, Kazakhstan and Tajikistan.[23] The organization clearly helps to bolster Russia's military role in the CIS and thus reinforces its military position in all three regions of the Near Abroad that we identify.

THE SHANGHAI COOPERATION ORGANIZATION

Putin is much more ambivalent about the Shanghai Cooperation Organization (SCO), which he was instrumental in founding in collaboration with
China, than about the CSTO. This organization grew out of a group of five
countries which the then-Foreign Minister Evgeny Primakov brought together in 1996. Dubbed "The Shanghai Five," the group included China and three
of the five Central Asian states (Kyrgyzstan, Kazakhstan, and Tajikistan, all
on the border with China). Its declared purpose was to assist in the resolution
of border disputes and facilitate border demilitarization among its members.
With Putin's encouragement, this group added Uzbekistan to its numbers and
formed the Shanghai Cooperation Organization in 2001.[24] Sixteen years later, India and Pakistan were welcomed into its ranks, also on Putin's urging.[25]
Since then its focus has broadened to include regional security cooperation,
counter-terrorism activities, intelligence sharing and economic cooperation
of various kinds.

Putin's vision for the SCO evolved in the first years after its founding. As
we have seen in Chapter 1, in the aftermath of NATO's expansion into the
Baltics in 2004, Putin became more and more concerned about the threat
NATO posed to Russia's security. The largest single expansion of the EU
occurred in the same year. That included not only the Baltic States, but also
four countries that had been part of the Soviet alliance system.[26] This added
to Putin's sense that Russian dominance of the Near Abroad was being
challenged. These events were followed by the Orange Revolution in
Ukraine. Putin must have become alarmed by the possibility that Western-
assisted democratic regime change in the Near Abroad could spark similar
developments in Russia that might threaten his own power and that of his
government. The SCO seemed to offer something of an answer to all of these
concerns. A regional bloc that included China would constitute a new pole of
power in the international system, one that could eventually rival or balance
the power of NATO and the EU.[27] As Putin saw it, we believe, such a bloc
could serve as an instrument for enhancing Russian power in Central Asia
and help to prevent Western sponsored regime change there.[28] At the same
time, the SCO could advance Putin's objectives of preventing the flow of
terrorists and narcotics across Russia's borders.[29] In the early years, therefore, Putin seemed eager to promote the political, military, and economic
power of this new organization and championed cooperation among its members in all of these spheres. As time passed, however, the Russian President

seems to have become wary of China's growing role in Central Asia and thus of its role in the SCO. In recent years he sought as much to limit that role as to enhance the power of that organization.

The SCO does seem to have stimulated some regional cooperation. Its yearly summits provide a useful forum for the exchange of views and diffusion of tensions among the members—a necessary condition for cooperation among independent states. Shared concerns are regularly aired, especially the situation in Afghanistan. The SCO has also provided a mechanism for military cooperation. It holds regular military exercises, usually involving several thousand Russian and Chinese troops, with representatives of the other members participating as observers. Its Regional Anti-Terrorist Structure facilitates intelligence sharing among the members and closely monitors both Islamist activities on the internet and the return or relocation to Afghanistan of militants from Iraq, Syria, and elsewhere, as well as movement of terrorists across the Afghan border into Central Asia and China. Over the years it has sometimes served Russia's interests by providing diplomatic backing for its policy positions, such as its opposition to U.S. missile defense programs. With the addition of India and Pakistan, the organization now represents a far larger territorial and demographic base than NATO or the EU, and as Putin recently boasted, the combined purchasing power of its members exceeds that of the G-7 (which ejected Russia after its annexation of Crimea). It has thus become a potential pole of power in the international system, as Putin has hoped. In other words, the SCO has contributed to the achievement of some of Putin's goals for it.

However, one should not exaggerate its accomplishments from Putin's point of view. Its military potential has been limited by the fact that it has no troops of its own, and military coordination among its members does not seem to extend beyond the staging of large exercises. Despite the agreement of all participants on the dangers emanating from Afghanistan, the SCO has never deployed troops there, leaving that task to NATO. While it arguably represents the world's largest market, the SCO does little to promote trade among its members. Although China, its chief source of capital, has used SCO summits to announce its plans to invest in the economies of the other members,[30] few of those funds have been channeled through SCO itself. Rather, Beijing arranges its investments bilaterally or through other mechanisms such as its Belt and Road Initiative (BRI) or the Asian Infrastructure Investment Bank (AIIB) which it initiated in 2014.[31] Nor has Putin always obtained the support he wanted from the SCO. On some important occasions, fellow members have declined to back his policies. After Russia's 2008 invasion of Georgia, for example, they refused to join in recognizing the independence of South Ossetia and Abkhazia, hitherto part of that country. Instead, they called on all parties in the Caucasus to resolve "existing problems" through dialogue and negotiation, not the use of force.

The limited accomplishments of the SCO are in part the consequence of its lack of funds. The Central Asian members are candidates for assistance, rather than potential investors, and they are just as happy to accept loans from China directly or participate in the BRI.[32] They have all joined the Chinese-sponsored AIIB and receive assistance from China through that mechanism. Russia has lacked the resources to make comparably large investments in Central Asia, either bilaterally or through the SCO. Thus as Richard Weitz has aptly put it, that organization is "chronically underfunded."[33]

Also constraining the activity of the SCO are the divergent perspectives of its members on what its ultimate purpose should be. The Russian President may want the organization to counter the power of NATO and the EU. China is much more concerned with America's military presence and activity in the Pacific than with NATO forces in Europe and is content to have the United States invest in bolstering NATO's strength rather than in modernizing its naval and other deployments in East Asia. The People's Republic is eager to do business with the EU, rather than compete with it. India has an excellent relationship with the United States and is not interested in combatting perceived American hegemony.

Longstanding territorial and other strategic conflicts also hamper cooperation among the members of the SCO, especially as its ranks have grown. As long as their bitter dispute over Kashmir continues, India and Pakistan are unlikely to want to engage in joint military operations. India and China have not resolved their border conflict, and India's nuclear arsenal was created to counter China's. It is hard to imagine these two powers coordinating a military operation.

The relationship between Russia and China, the founders of the SCO, is far more complicated. Despite steadily increasing Chinese investments in Russia and similarly expanding military cooperation between the two powers, in recent years Putin has become sensitive to China's growing influence in Central Asia and has not wanted the SCO to reinforce that influence. China's financial activity in Central Asia has been a particular worry to Russia. Beijing's Belt and Road Initiative (BRI) is a vast global undertaking involving construction of roads, railroads, pipelines and modernized border crossings designed to link China economically with Europe, South Asia, the Middle East and (by sea) with Africa and Latin America.[34] Total investment may well exceed $1 trillion in the next decade.[35] Central Asia is a key component of this project—perhaps the most important—since China's overland trade with Europe and South Asia must traverse the region. The plan was first announced in Kazakhstan in 2013, and much of the money already invested has been directed there in the last decade. With a large (but declining) current account surplus and reserves, economists believe that China can afford these kinds of expenditures,[36] but Russia cannot begin to match them.

China's investments in Central Asia, initiated even before the BRI was proclaimed, have begun to pay off. Chinese trade with the Near Abroad was estimated at $46 billion in 2016, less than Russia's but growing faster. As of 2016 Kazakhstan was sending some four-hundred-thousand barrels of oil daily to China, which has a deficit in fossil fuels. By 2020 the gas pipelines from Central Asia to China will be expected to supply about 40 percent of China's needs. Considering China's enormous population and concern to develop its western provinces, the demand for food, energy, and fuels is sure to attract the attention of Central Asian countries suffering from reduced oil and gas profits. Even though the Chinese have been careful not to intervene in Central Asian political changes and to cultivate good relations with Putin's regime, Chinese actions have clearly been troubling for Moscow because an economic relationship of this scale can readily translate into political influence (this issue is discussed further in Chapter 7).

As a result, Putin has blocked Chinese initiatives aimed at strengthening the economic role and impact of the SCO. At its 2015 summit, member states adopted a SCO Development Strategy to strengthen regional financial, investment and trade cooperation. Although Putin backed the plan rhetorically, he has vetoed China's proposal of an inter-SCO Development Bank as a vehicle for implementing it. Reportedly he feared that China would dominate such an institution as it has the AIIB.[37] He has likewise opposed China's repeated attempts to create a free trade zone encompassing all the members of the SCO. The Russian President would have to view such a zone as a threat to Russian exports to Central Asia. Instead, he has sought to strengthen the EaEU by establishing a customs union with a common external tariff against imports from China.[38] We discuss this further in Chapter 7.

This analysis suggests that while the SCO has served Russian interests in some respects, it has fallen short of fulfilling Putin's expansive hopes and has posed a challenge to Putin's ambitions in the Near Abroad. Its most significant contribution has probably been in the sphere of counter-terrorism, for which it has created an institutional mechanism. It is considering a comparable mechanism devoted to combatting drug-trafficking and thus may be of comparable help to Russia in that sphere in the future.[39] It may have been of some assistance to Putin in preventing regime change in the region, probably through the exchange of ideas and information among the leaders attending the annual summits. Those meetings give him an opportunity to articulate and defend his policy positions and in so doing may help to bolster Russian influence in the Central Asian portion of the Near Abroad. Interactions with other heads of state and their staffs may also aid the Russian President by enabling him to monitor Chinese economic expansion in the region. However, it is hard to argue that the SCO has achieved the status of a major pole of power in the international system on a par with NATO. Were China and Russia to coordinate their military capabilities in the context of the SCO, the resulting force would contain more than three million active duty personnel; the combined ballistic missile force would be the world's largest. Adding the capabilities of Indian and Pakistan to the package would create an organization presiding over four nuclear-armed military establishments and millions of additional troops. However, in the light of the enmities and rivalries discussed above, such an outcome is unlikely in the extreme. The ability of the SCO to advance Putin's policy goals in the Near Abroad is therefore quite limited.

THE EURASIAN ECONOMIC UNION

Another Russian-led multilateral effort is to regulate trade with the Near Abroad, on terms favorable to Moscow. Kazakhstan's ex-President Nursultan Nazarbaev had long championed some kind of Eurasian economic community. After several false starts, a Russia-Kazakhstan-Belarus customs union began to operate in 2009–2010, but progress was slow even for that alignment, as concessions and exceptions had to be made. In 2010 Putin announced in *Izvestia* his plan for a new "European Union" that would rival the European Union in scope and economic strength. This entity soon became the Eurasian *Economic* Union (EaEU) in deference to objections by Kazakhstan and Belarus to political integration. The EaEU has had diverse and ambitious objectives on paper, including a customs union with a common external tariff. It has a single set of regulations for movement of labor and capital and a supranational forum, although no real enforcement power.[40] By 2016 membership in the EaEU included Kyrgyzstan and Armenia, besides the original three states.

If Moscow has its way, the expanded EaEU will be a monetary union as well, with the ruble a single regional currency, instead of dollars or euros. As European Union experience shows, however, a single currency would require monetary and fiscal conformity—a bridge too far even for the West Europeans! Even free passage of capital as well as all goods and services will not suffice to create a true monetary union. Nor will such provisions actually generate much investment, and to date little has occurred through the EaEU channel.[41]

Progress toward implementing Putin's vision has been slow. In 2015 Nazarbaev warned against accepting new members or deepening integration. Aware of a trade imbalance to the disadvantage of Kazakhstan, he called for "simplification and liberalization" of the customs code to allow Kazakhstan easier access to the Russian energy market.[42] The Western sanctions and counter-sanctions of 2014—and the resulting depreciation of the Russian ruble in 2015—caused considerable difficulties.[43] Not surprisingly, with the energy price collapse during the 2014 downturn, intra-EaEU trade fell by 11 percent. Reportedly only a fraction of the numerous border restrictions have been removed, with others likely "soon." Possibly because of Nazarbaev's understandable preference for open trade with China, not a member of the EaEU, completion of the common market has now been postponed to 2025.

Direction of trade under the EaEU tariffs would appear to be a significant benefit for the Putin regime, not only because of fees at collection points in Russia. Protection offers extra profits for several Russian manufacturers— for example, producers of automobiles and trucks. Adopting the Russian external tariffs, which apply to all imports, has meant that the duty on automobiles rose from 10 percent to 30–35 percent or more on used vehicles. This protection favors Russian-made vehicles over preferred European brands. Such profits to Putin's elite managers and owners would be a major benefit to fortify his regime.

How would this EaEU work in eventual practice outside Russia? Common markets everywhere usually create negative trade diversion from cheaper sources, and that is highly likely in this case. This effect, as well as delays at the borders, has inevitably had a depressing impact on trade.[44] To conform to the EaEU protocols Kazakhstan had to increase some 45 percent in its tariff rates. Because the Russian tariff imposed on Kazakhstan makes automobiles from Japan, South Korea, and elsewhere far more expensive, well-off Kazakhstanis have been unhappy with the results of the customs union. For Kazakhstanis, for example, the price of a Toyota Camry went from $22,000 to $40,000! They may well resent the clear attempt to make Russian Ladas competitive, despite their notoriously poor quality. Even in the previous customs union prices of leather and medicines also rose very noticeably, provoking indignation among consumers in Kazakhstan. Supposedly the EaEU does want to develop a "partnership with China," but meanwhile the active trade with China (or Iran) is being obstructed as a way of favoring less attractive exports from Russia.[45] According to Bola Abilov, Co-chairman of the Kazakh oppositionist social democratic party Azat, the tariffs (and sanctions on and by Russia) have also made food and fuel much more expensive. For example, Kazakhstan limits imports of cheaper Kyrgyz potatoes on the ground of inadequate sanitary oversight. This is how trade diversion works against EaEU consumers. Any way it gets through, though. Chinese trade with the nearby five Central Asian economies had grown from $50 billion already in 2013, showing its potential.[46]

The EaEU protectionism must have a political rationale, rather than a strictly material one, because a customs union everywhere works best when trade with the outside world is free and competitive. If important states like Uzbekistan, China, and South Korea are not included, the benefits are reduced. Meanwhile, though, a larger internal market can induce economies of scale for customs union customers. However, regional cooperation in the post-Soviet world of authoritarian states has always been unreliable, even if useful to leaders whose elite supporters stand to benefit.

OTHER MULTILATERAL INSTITUTIONS IN EURASIA

Not all the multilateral institutions and activities promoted by Russia require treaties or political commitments. The Russian Orthodox Church, headquartered in Moscow, operates Russian World (Russki Mir), which promotes conservative moral values in open conferences throughout the region.[47] Patriarch Kirill I of Moscow (2009–present) has been a strong supporter of Putin and Russian civilization, even beyond the Russian Federation. Until recently the Russian patriarch had a role in appointing clerics through the Near Abroad, but now the authorities in Istanbul have allowed the Ukrainian Orthodox Church to split off from Moscow (autocephaly).

Russian television and radio are widely broadcast to Russian-speaking populations of Kazakhstan, Kyrgyzstan, Belarus, and the Baltic states. According to a 2014 Gallup poll, two-thirds of the Kazakhstani audience considered the radio program "Sputnik" to be "reliable," though its content is very much the Kremlin line.[48] On Russian channels, for example, all the "color revolutions" of Georgia, Ukraine, and Kyrgyzstan are attributed to American instigation. *Rossotrudnichestvo* and other social websites are also well distributed.[49] By contrast, efforts and spending by the European Union and the United States in Russia's Near Abroad –for example, outlays for Radio Liberty and Voice of America broadcasting in the region-- have been slight, compared with military aid from the West.

Russia's educational efforts have increased under Putin. There are science and cultural centers in many Central Asian cities teaching the Russian language. Some 150,000 Central Asians study in Russia, about a third of them on Russian Federation scholarships. In Tajikistan, where the local language is Tajik with Russian used for business, twenty-eight teachers of Russian have been engaged and sixty thousand Russian textbooks have been distributed recently. Plans have been approved to build schools in five cities to teach in Russian.[50] Such schools have been opened in Turkmenistan, financed by Gazprom, and in Bishkek, Kyrgyzstan, backed by the Russian Peace Foundation. A convention of Russian "Compatriots" (pro-Russian foreigners) meets regularly, usually in Moscow. They receive guidelines from Moscow regarding their agendas.[51]

Not least in importance, Russia's embassies in the Near Abroad look after the interests of Russian citizens, as do the foreign services of all major countries. Among other things, Russian diplomats advise Moscow of developments in their postings, and thus assist in all the other means of influence Russia has through its multilateral organizations.

CONCLUSION AND LOOK AHEAD

We have described Russia's current efforts to organize its neighborhood as intended to protect and enhance Putin's great power ambition. It is hard to know whether Russian soft power, as exercised through various attempts to shape public attitudes and opinions, contributes significantly to solidifying Russian influence and control in the Near Abroad. Very likely, it does. The formal multilateral institutions the President has promoted cannot really rival their western counterparts, although the demographic base of the SCO far exceeds that of any European or trans-Atlantic organization. However, all four of the institutions we discuss provide opportunities for Putin and other Russian officials to interact and exchange ideas with their counterparts in the Near Abroad and monitor Chinese activity there. Such activities do help to maintain the region as Russia's sphere of influence, even if there have been some very significant defections. The CSTO and the EaEU are unlikely to attract many new members and will not serve to unite the Near Abroad under Russia's leadership, as Putin hoped. However, both organizations may achieve a somewhat higher level of integration than exists today. The SCO appears to have the greatest potential to grow. Armenia and Azerbaijan are potential members, and even more remote Belarus has expressed an interest. Officially neutral Turkmenistan appears to prefer participating as a "Guest Attendee." At least seven countries outside the Near Abroad already participate in SCO meetings as non-voting "observers" or "dialogue partners."[52] Iran has applied for membership, and Turkey has declared that it wants to join.[53] In other words, while this institution is unlikely ever to incorporate the entire range of countries Russia claims as properly in its sphere, the SCO may help to enhance Russia's status beyond that sphere.

NOTES

1. The Baltic States refused.

2. Gabrielle Tetrault-Farber, "CIS Countries Neutral on Crimea Annexation," *The Moscow Times*, March 18, 2014.

3. Irina Khalip, *Nezavisimaia Gazeta,* July 12, 2017. CD 69, no. 28: 10.

4. Vladimir Zharikin, "Institute of CIS countries," *Izvestia*, April 12, 2016.

5. *Johnson's Russia List*, October 5, 2011.

6. Alexey Eremenko, "Ukraine Leaving CIS Shoots Down Kremlin's Imperial Ambitions, *The Moscow Times*, May 27, 2014.

7. As mentioned in Chapter 1, Note 8, the members include three of the five Central Asian States (Kazakhstan, Kyrgyzstan, and Tajikistan), as well as Armenia and Belarus, along with the Russian Federation. As one might imagine, these are Russia's closest and most (although not always) cooperative allies in the Near Abroad.

8. Nikolai Bordyzha, CSTO Secretary General at the time, declared that "events in North Africa have opened our eyes." Quoted in J. Berkshere Miller, "Russia Launches Wargames," *The Diplomat*, September 23, 2011.

9. Isabelle Facon, "Moscow's Global Foreign and Security Policy," *Asian Security* 53, no. 3 (May-June, 2013): 461–83.

10. "Why Russia's Military Alliance Is Not the Next NATO," *Stratfor*, January 10, 2017.

11. In 2009, in the context of a dispute with Moscow, Belarussian President Alexander Lukashenko challenged President Medvedev: "Why should my men fight in Kazakhstan? Mothers would ask me why I sent their sons to fight so far from Belarus. For what?" Quoted in

Nikolaus von Twickel, "Lukashenko Plays Coy with Kremlin," *The Moscow Times*, August 28, 2009.

12. "Bordyuzha: CSTO ready to deploy its peacekeepers to resolve conflict in Ukraine," *Belarus News*, April 2, 2015.

13. Joshua Kucera, "CSTO Ready, But Not Yet Willing, to Send Troops to Syria," *Eurasianet*, December 1, 2017; Aleksandr Golts, "Russia's Allies Do Not Want to Take Part in Syrian Operation," *Eurasia Daily Monitor* 15, no. 96 (June 21, 2018).

14. Vladimir Mukhin, *Nezavisimaia Gazeta,* September 16, 2015.

15. Stephen Blank, "A Sino-Uzbek Axis in Central Asia?" *Central Asia-Caucasus Analyst* 12, no. 16 (September 1, 2010). In this instance Belarus was critical of Russia for its failure to mobilize the CSTO to intervene.

16. "Uzbekistan Suspends Its Membership in CSTO," *Gazette of Central Asia*, June 29, 2012.

17. Fozil Mashrab, "Russia Tacitly Entices Uzbekistan with Benefits of EEU and CSTO Membership," *Eurasia Daily Monitor* 14, no. 149 (November 17, 2017).

18. However, the new President of Uzbekistan, Shavkat Mirziyoyev agreed to join in CSTO military exercises in mountainous conditions and has stepped up military cooperation with Moscow on a variety of fronts. Mirziyoyev does not seem as wary of Russia as his predecessor was. "Uzbekistan and Russia: Chilly Weather, Warm Relations," *Eurasianet*, October 17, 2018.

19. Yelena Chernenko in *Kommersant*, November 2, 2011. Translated in Johnson's Russia List, November 3, 2011. The new head of the CSTO is Yuri Khachaturov, an Armenian general.

20. A "major arms procurement program" was announced by the CSTO in 2014. www. CNSnews.com, April 30, 2017.

21. Roger Mac Dermott, "Russia Rehearses Military Intervention in Central Asia and the Caucasus," *The Central Asia-Caucasus Analyst*, November 17, 2017.

22. See, for example, Elena Kropotcheva, "Russian and the Collective Security Organization: Multilateral Policy of Unilateral Ambition," *Europe-Asia Studies*, November 25, 2016: 1526–52.

23. "Why Russia's Military Alliance Is Not the Next NATO," *Stratfor*, January 10, 2017.

24. As we have seen with regard to the CIS, Turkmenistan has consistently sought to limit its involvement with any multilateral institutions and has generally remained outside them.

25. China, whose relationship with India has never been entirely amicable, initially resisted but eventually changed its mind.

26. Hungary, Poland, the Czech Republic, and Slovakia.

27. This had been the vision of Primakov, who has been called "the ideological godfather of Putinism." Samuel Ramani, "Yevgeny Primakov—The Ideological Godfather of Putinism," *Modern Diplomacy,* June 30, 2015.

28. Richard Weitz, "The Shanghai Cooperation Organization (SCO): Rebirth and Regeneration?–Analysis," *Eurasia Review*, October 10, 2014.

29. Eleanor Albert, "The Shanghai Cooperation Organization," Council on Foreign Relations, October 14, 2015. www.cfr.org/backgrounder/shanghai-cooperation-organization

30. For example, at a SCO summit in Bishkek in September, 2013, Chinese President Xi Jinping pledged $50 billion for Central Asian infrastructure and energy projects.

31. One observer has suggested that the SCO as an organization has no military or economic effect in itself. Erica Marat, *The Military and the State in Central Asia* (London: Routledge 2010), 85.

32. China has emphasized pipeline construction and, more recently, transportation infrastructure. Road projects have already been approved for Kazakhstan (a capital ring road) and a toll road to Belarus. Investments at the Khorogos choke point at the border between China and Kazakhstan have allowed increased railroad traffic from there on to Europe. *The Economist*, July 2, 2016; George Voloshin, "Central Asia Ready to Follow China's Lead despite Russian Ties," *Eurasia Daily Monitor* 14, no. 71.

33. Richard Weitz, "The Shanghai Cooperation Organization's Growing Pains," *The Diplomat*, September 18, 2015.

34. Andrew Chatzky and James McBride, "China's Massive Belt and Road Initiative," Council on Foreign Relations, May 21, 2019. www.cfr.org/backgrounder/chinas-massive-belt-and-road-initiative .

35. Anja Manuel, "China Is Quietly Reshaping the World," *The Atlantic*, October 17, 2017.

36. *The Economist*, October 6, 2018.

37. Albert, "The Shanghai Cooperation Organization."

38. Weitz, "The Shanghai Cooperation Organization: Rebirth and Regeneration?"; Aleksandr Gabuev, "Taming the Dragon," *Russia in Global Affairs,* March 19, 2015.

39. Zhang Yan, "Anti-drug agency proposed for SCO," *China Daily*, June 6, 2018.

40. Bruno Maçães, *The Dawn of Eurasia* (New Haven, CT: Yale University Press, 2018), 187–89.

41. Arthur Gushkin, *Nezavisimaia.Gazeta.*, April 9, 2015. *CD* 67, no.15: 14.

42. Robert Donaldson and Vidya Nadkarni, *The Foreign Policy of Russia*, 6th ed. (Armonk, NY: Routledge, 2019), 178.

43. Evgeny Vinokurov, *Introduction to the Eurasian Economic Union* (London, UK: Palgrave Macmillan, 2018), 157.

44. Alexander Libman and Evgeny Vinokurov, *Holding Together Regionalism: Twenty Years of Post-Soviet Integration* (London, UK: Palgrave-Macmillan, 2012), 49. We are grateful to Richard Pomfret for this reference.

45. *Rossiiskaia gazeta*, June 1, 2016. CD 68, no. 22: 13.

46. Peter Leonard, "Economy and Sanctions Derail Russia's Central Asian Investments," *Eurasianet*, January 28, 2016 (quoting IMF figures).

47. Russian Orthodox Christianity rejects same-sex marriage, for instance.

48. N. Espinoza and J. Ray, "Information Wars: Ukraine and the West vs Russia and the West," *Harvard International Review*, May, 2016. In the Kyrgyz capital Bishkek, ten Russian television channels are received.

49. Established in 2008, *Rossotrudnichestvo* operates to maintain Russia's influence in the CIS, as well as in more than seventy other countries, to advance Russia's interests abroad. Soon after its founding, it received a budget of two billion rubles (over $30 million) with more promised for the future. *Sputnik International*, July 24, 2013.

50. According to Russian Foreign Minister Sergei Lavrov, *Rossiiskaia gazeta,* October 4, 2017. CD 69, no. 40: 14.

51. At the Fourth World Congress of Compatriots, Putin "stated that documents regarding Russian compatriot policy are no longer vague as 'support for the Russian diaspora is one of the most important policies of our state.'" Agnia Grigas, *Beyond Crimea*: *The New Russian Empire* (New Haven, CT: Yale, 2016), 91.

52. This was Turkey's response to the unanimous vote by the European Parliament to suspend accession negotiations with the EU.

53. "Fed up with EU, Turkey could join Shanghai bloc," *Reuters*, November 20, 2016.

Chapter Four

Bilateral Deals with Central Asian States

Given the complexity of multilateral action together with the different preferences of Putin's neighbors, the Kremlin has preferred bilateral arrangements that recognize the distinctive positions and variable strengths of the Central Asian countries that were once part of the USSR. At the same time each of these countries has tried to diversify support for its sovereignty and freedom of action by obtaining security resources, legitimacy, and development aid from all interested major powers, not just Russia.[1]

In this chapter we introduce five countries lying to the south of the Russian Federation by briefly analyzing their economic and demographic situations, their security arrangements, and Putin's efforts to assure their cooperation in achieving the five objectives outlined in Chapter 1. We conclude each section with a judgment about the success or failure of those efforts.

KAZAKHSTAN

We begin with the largest, strongest, and wealthiest of Russia's neighboring Central Asian states. Kazakhstan became a constituent republic of the USSR only in 1936, although the area had been a Russian-controlled khanate since the eighteenth century. Once President Putin was heard belittling the recent establishment of Kazakhstan's statehood, and some extremists in Moscow have called for reintegrating Kazakhstan into a revived Soviet Union, a vision rejected by most Kazakhs.

Demography

Of Kazakhstan's overall population of 18.5 million, some 63 percent are Kazakh in ethnicity and mostly Muslim. Ethnic Russians or Ukrainians constitute an estimated 23 percent.[2] Besides the Western Turkic language spoken in Kazakhstan,[3] Russian remains an official language. Many Russians live in the area immediately adjacent to the Russian Federation—a pattern unique in the Near Abroad—though quite a few of the richest ones live far away from the border area—in Karaganda, a center of extractive industries, the commercial center Almaty, and the new (since 1998) capital, Astana, recently renamed Nur-Sultan in honor of long-time President Nursultan Nazarbaev. Despite the prominence of Russians, ethnic Kazakhs are now given preference for governmental jobs, and this discrimination is resented by some Russians. Dual citizenship with Russia is not legal in Kazakhstan. To bolster the percentage of Kazakhs, returning nationals are granted rapid citizenship. Putin has pledged "active defense of the rights of Russians, our compatriots . . . by all available means and [their] self-defense."[4] Despite their resentments, the Russians in Kazakhstan are not clamoring for such measures to be implemented. The resident Russian population still seems "quiet and calm," according to a well-informed visitor.[5]

Economy

In 2018 Kazakhstan's gross national product per capita was $26,300,[6] making it an "upper middle income" country. Kazakhstan's prime export is crude oil, though the country also produces uranium, coal, iron ore, and various minerals. In 2015 the country exported some 66 million tons of oil, which was about 84 percent of its production. That is just two percent of the world's supply but twelve percent of the CIS total.

International energy companies have been active in promoting Kazakhstan's petroleum expansion. Western companies helped in exploiting geologically difficult fields, but Lukoil and Rosneft have also been present. Now, perhaps owing to the price decline, as well as gas leaks, the promising Kashagan field output had to be interrupted from 2013–2016. By 2012 China's state-owned National Petroleum Company produced a fifth of all Kazakhstan's oil output. With Chinese interests now owning some of Kazakhstan's oil fields, purchased at a cost of $5 billion, Beijing was called on to lend that financially troubled country a further $5 billion.[7] In 2017 Kazakhstan had to relinquish its 49 percent stake in the critical Khorgos railroad link from China.

The Russian Transneft and Lukoil pipelines carry much Kazakh oil; one route circumvents Ukraine to reach Black Sea ports. The Caspian Sea Convention of 2018 may provide an additional outlet for Kazakhstani natural gas. Rosneft pumps some of it to China, which now takes some 22 percent of the total, as against only 9 percent sold to Russia.

In all, from 1990 until 2015 Kazakhstan received $152 billion in foreign direct investment. The amount was much higher ($250 billion) in the more recent shorter period from 2009–2018.[8] By now China has invested more than $40 billion there. Kazakhstan's coal and electricity sector has been attractive for some Russian investors, along with communications and uranium mining.[9] Most of the largest enterprises are state-owned; smaller firms still falter, despite a favorable business climate, and some skilled workers think of leaving.[10] Of its enormous area only 11 percent of Kazakhstan is arable though much of this land is available. Most recently, increasing amounts of grain and soybeans have been sent to China as partial replacement of American shipments.

Though Kazakhstan did recover in 2018, the lower oil prices of 2015-17 affected its prosperity by increasing unemployment, which is still nearly 5 percent.[11] When the oil price collapsed, it affected Russia, Kazakhstan's main direct customer, and Kazakhstan suffered a 37 percent fall in the value of its external trade. The shortage of export revenues forced a devaluation of the Kazakh *tenge* by 45 percent against the dollar and an increase in the official interest rate to 17 percent—both more drastic than the Russian adjustment. The energy company KazMunaigaz had to resort to help from the country's national bank, while the country's accumulated strategic reserve fund helped local businesses with other deficiencies. In 2016 a stimulus plan worth $9 billion was required.[12] A decline in the value of the Russian ruble in 2018 was accompanied by a further 15 percent depreciation of the Kazakh *tenge* currency. For the local economy, the resulting higher import prices meant lower retail sales and real incomes.

During the oil-price recession, the "deteriorating social economic situation" threatened domestic instability in Kazakhstan. According to the National Security Commission, some 450 Kazakhstanis joined ISIS during that time.[13] Most vulnerable have been oil workers in the west of the country. They are essential to this vital industry and sometimes have protested their pay and conditions. When that happened before, top government officials would press foreign companies to concede; if the concessions were not sufficient, police actions were resorted to. A terrorist attack in July 2016 was unexpected; twenty-five people, including the Islamist assailants, were killed. People complained to foreign journalists about "unemployment, low wages, corruption, and lack of access to housing, health care and education."[14] However, based on our visits and conversations, there didn't seem to be enough dissent in this vast country to require armed Russian security assistance. Now stability has returned.

Relations with the Russian Federation

Overall control over Kazakhstan's politics had long been in the hands of Nazarbaev, a former Soviet official and the country's only President from 1990 until 2019, when he resigned from that post. He remains head of the Security Council and much else, though his loyal supporter Kassym-Zhomart Tokayev has been chosen to serve the remainder of his term. Mr. Tokayev promises stability. Nazarbaev's Nur Otan party has always held a dominant position in the country's parliament. His frequent policy proclamations were generally accepted as authoritative, even though "public space for dissent [was] closed."[15] Nazarbaev was generally friendly to Russia, although he did not support the annexation of Crimea in February, 2014. To be sure, Russian Foreign Minister Sergei Lavrov denied any potential Kazakhstani parallel to the case of Crimea, but the Kazakhstani leadership was probably not reassured.

Kazakhstan is a member of all of the principal multilateral institutions Russia has created to bolster its great power status: the CIS, the CSTO, the SCO, and the EaEU (see Chapter 3). Kazakhstan collects intelligence and conducts joint anti-terrorism and anti-drug smuggling exercises with the six members of these organizations with which it shares common borders. The Cosmodrome space launch center at Baikonur is rented to Russia for $115 million yearly.

Even with its early memberships in the EaEU and the other multilateral institutions, however, Nazarbaev's policy moves demonstrated that his country does not want to become a Russian colony. Like most of the other Central Asian states, Kazakhstan participates in NATO's Partnerships for Peace. An "Enhanced Partnership and Cooperation" agreement with the EU was signed in November, 2015. The country became a full member of the World Trade Organization as of November 2016. NATO and UN soldiers (*without* Russia) recently participated in KAZBAT "Steppe Eagle" exercises near Almaty.

The United States has been financing a biological warfare center since 2016 in Almaty.

Even with a small defense budget, Kazakhstan has had the means to renovate its 39,000-member armed forces by buying helicopters and armored vehicles, for example, at Russian domestic "bargain" prices.[16] Its S300 missiles were obtained to support a unified air defense system with Moscow. But Kazakhstan has also been interested in security support from China and the West, not only Russia.[17] So Nazarbaev purchased helicopters of American and European types. Besides the hardware acquisition, the country sends military cadets to both Russia and China.

The Yelbasy or "National Leader," as Nazarbaev liked to be called, showed interest in non-Russian social and economic models, too. Malaysia, a majority Islamic state in south Asia that has embraced "Islamic finance," was studied for use in Kazakhstan as another indicator of its independent legitimacy.[18] To attract Islamic finance for its banking sector, he involved the Islamic Development Bank (IDB), which is supported from Dubai. Nazarbaev also authorized a transition to English instruction in schools and universities. The new financial hub in Astana (now Nur-Sultan) will operate on the basis of English law.

Not all of Kazakhstan's efforts to assert its independent position on the world stage have proved worthwhile. Attendance at Astana's elaborate EXPO-2017, said to have cost $3 billion, was disappointing. A recent proposal to allow foreigners (likely Chinese) to lease Kazakhstani land failed, owing to wide-spread suspicion of Chinese economic influence in the country. But some shuttle trade at the promising Khorogos dryport transit district is permitted, even though Russia discourages this activity.[19]

Considering his willing cooperation with many Russian projects, such as the EaEU and the CSTO, Nazarbaev's stable regime and that of his successor hardly threaten Putin's dominance in Central Eurasia. For instance, Kazakhstan readily agreed to the provision of the 2018 Caspian Sea Convention which excludes military or naval activities on the inland sea from outside powers. However, China's steadily growing influence in Kazakhstan's economy and security establishment poses a growing challenge to Russian dominance.

UZBEKISTAN

With about 30 million residents, mostly of Uzbek or Tajik ethnicity, Uzbekistan has the largest population of all the Central Asian countries. A double-landlocked country, it borders all the other ex-Soviet states in the region except Russia. Tashkent, its large capital (with 2.5 million people), was the administrative center of the region in Soviet times. The historic cities of Bukhara and Samarkand also attract tourists to their famous medieval Muslim sites. Though Uzbek, a Turkic language, is written in a Latin alphabet, Russian is spoken among officials, and some twenty-five thousand young Uzbeks are students in Russia.

Economy

Uzbekistan's GDP per capita for 2018 was $6900—noticeably less than its larger northern neighbors. Uzbekistan's reported GDP growth of 6 percent may be exaggerated, as it fails to allow for the country's chronic inflation rates of over 10 percent.

Though it is not a member of the EaEU, Uzbekistan sells much of its abundant natural gas (3.3 billion cubic meters in 2015) north to Russia through its main gas pipeline (CAC). In 2016 Gazprom agreed to buy 4 billion cubic meters of gas from the Uzbekistanis. However, Uzbekistan transmits more than twice that amount (10 billion cubic meters) of its gas to China. Uzbekistan also exports gold, uranium, and many other metals to global markets. Its world-class cotton production still depends on some coerced labor and on its control of irrigation waters from rivers that rise in Kyrgyzstan and Tajikistan. The country is self-sufficient in food with plentiful fruits and vegetables in its farmers' markets. Textiles and machinery are also produced by its balanced economy. Uzbekistan has exported GM Nexia automobiles to Russia, although the energy-price depression, together with the EaEU's protection, threatens this trade.

Even without a border with the Russian Federation, nearly three and one half million Uzbek citizens work seasonally in Russia (or Kazakhstan). However, because Uzbekistan has declined EaEU membership, its migrant laborers probably lose out on some jobs to Kyrgyz competitors who enter Russia freely. During the energy-price depression, the dollar value of Uzbekistan's remittances fell in 2015 to some $3.06 billion, around half of the amount taken out of Russia in 2013–2014, according to the Russian Central Bank.[20] Russian-Uzbek trade also fell in 2015–2016, though Uzbekistan's well-known fruit and vegetables still found markets in Siberia. As a result of these developments, the official exchange rate for the Uzbek *som* had to be devalued by 25 percent from its previous rate. Dollars at a higher price were usually obtainable at outdoor markets, however.

Relations with the Russian Federation

Long suspicious of Russian initiatives in the political and military arenas, Uzbekistan's autocratic President Islam Karimov (who died in September 2016) had nevertheless welcomed Moscow's interest in developing Uzbekistan's petroleum reserves and communications facilities. Gas sales continued, too, as the Russian firm OAO Lukoil negotiated a deal in 2004 to develop additional gas fields. Russian companies are still active investors in Uzbekistan.

Uzbekistan has had some off-and-on security cooperation with the CSTO and also with NATO, but Karimov warned that foreign bases would no longer be welcome in Uzbekistan.[21] Nor would Uzbekistani troops be used outside the country, for example, to fight ISIS.[22] Like its neighbors, Uzbekistan has been wary of Islamist armed interventions, but Tashkent resisted CSTO assistance in armed clashes between Uzbeks and terrorists of the Islamic Movement of Uzbekistan (IMU). Thus the Karimov regime imprisoned or exiled most suspected Islamist leaders. Mosque imams and Muslim associations were watched for any possible political dissent. Despite these security concerns, President Karimov generally assumed a more independent posture from Russia. He was critical of the Crimean annexation and Ukrainian intervention. In his last trip to Moscow, Karimov demanded payment of an estimated $865 million for the jewels and other valuables taken by Russian forces from his country during the Bolshevik Revolution and its aftermath. The Duma apparently agreed to most of that.

Uzbekistan is also associated with NATO's Partnership for Peace as well as the Organization of Security and Cooperation in Eurasia (OSCE), though it always resisted that organization's offers of scrutiny in its flawed elections. The Partnership for Peace is a program to improve military interoperability, defense planning, and modern budgeting. Use of NATO facilities to attain these goals is apparently discretionary.

There is no evidence that Karimov's successor, President Shavkat Mirziyoyev, who worked closely with him, will change Uzbekistan's preference for independence if it can be assured without a sacrifice of modest economic and technological progress.[23] The new President has been slow to name all his leadership team owing to the shortage of experienced personnel. He did fire the former minister of finance, Rustam Azimov, who functioned as prime minister under Karimov. The new Prime Minister is Abdulla Aripov, a former deputy prime minister who had been out of power from 2012 to 2016. Besides two sons-in-law placed in the administration, Mirziyoyev seems be interested in promoting economic technocrats, even from abroad, and gently reducing the power of security *siloviki.*[24] Some political prisoners have been released, and most of those on a previous security watch list have been removed from it. More important, Mirziyoyev has lifted the official restrictions on the *som* currency and has reduced tariffs. Negotiations to join the World Trade Organization have been resumed, and Europe's EBRD has returned to Tashkent for business.

Recognizing Uzbekistan's role in security for the region, President Putin visited the new President, bringing a reported $15 billion in proposals, including a nuclear power station near Bukhara estimated to cost $11 billion. Uzbekistan will also buy new weapons from Russia at reduced prices.

China's Involvement

China responded to this new activity with a plan to build a railway from Khorgos to the Fergana Valley and other projects for $20 billion.[25] Uzbekistan endorses the Chinese-initiated the BRI (the new Silk Road), as well as the projects of the Asian Development Bank to develop trade zones to promote trans-Asian commerce. The Chinese telecomm companies Huawei and ZTE have relocated assembly plants in Uzbekistan. Recently China announced it will fund a synthetic fuel plant there. Uzbekistan has of course long been open to Chinese goods coming through Kyrgyzstan via private traders.

Uzbekistan has long had active relations with South Korea and Japan, too. South Korean firms have made significant investments everywhere in Central Asia. Not long ago the Republic of Korea announced it will lend Uzbekistan $30 million for an information technology and education project. Korea Resources Corporation will mine uranium, iron, and gold in the country, according to *The Korea Herald*. South Korea will also develop the Surgil gas field jointly with Uzbekistan and build a chemical plant nearby, at an estimated cost of $3 billion. Korea's branded consumer goods are popular throughout the region, and both India and Japan are trying to do more business there, too. Foreign universities operate to supplement Uzbekistan's weak ones. All these connections dilute Russia's influence.

In sum, Uzbekistan has long assumed a balanced or "multi-vectoral" position, hoping to profit from all outsiders without serious breach of its independence and freedom of maneuver.[26] For Uzbekistan as well as Kazakhstan, "multi-vector" does involve definite obligations and prudential policy. Some view it as a disguise for changes of orientation by authoritarian rulers depending on opportunity and constraints.[27] So long as the new regime can control its few dissenters, Putin does not need to worry about democratic regime change in Tashkent. With time, China's growing economic role in the country, as in Kazakhstan, is likely to pose the most serious threat to Russian dominance.

KYRGYZSTAN

The small and poor Kyrgyz Republic is largely covered by the Tien Shan and Pamir mountains, which divide the country between the Chui region of the north and the agrarian Osh region of the south, with its considerable Uzbek population. A modern highway, built by the Chinese, connects these halves. Though about half of Russian and other Slavic officials and families emigrated after 1991, Russian-speakers and Orthodox believers are still very noticeable in the bustling capital of Bishkek in the north. Kyrgyz-speakers benefit from employment preferences.

Economy

Having barely recovered from the post-Soviet disruptions of the 1990s, the current GDP of $3,700 per capita in Kyrgyzstan reflects slow advances since 2000 and out-migration which exceeds natural population growth. Chronic unemployment is today around 7 to 8 percent. More than a quarter of all Kyrgyzstanis are engaged in cotton or vegetable agriculture and animal husbandry on the six percent of the land which is arable. A large share of the national income of the country comes from remittances from the several hundred thousand Kyrgyz working in Russia who contributed at least $2–3 billion yearly from 2013–2017.[28] This source of revenue is somewhat shaky as Central Asian migrants are not popular in Russia and are less needed in the near stagnation of the economy there since 2015. Kyrgyzstan does export gold from a Canadian-operated mine (nearly exhausted) and some metals from the mountains. To be sure, there are some small food processing industries. When Uzbekistan discontinued previously supplied natural gas supplies to nearby Kyrgyzstan for failure to pay, Gazprom took over Kyrgyzgaz pipelines in 2014 for a symbolic amount and has announced a major expansion of gas distribution throughout the country over the next decade.[29] Some hydropower comes to Kyrgyzstan from the Naryn River, on which the huge new Karabata dam was to be built by Russia at a cost of $2 billion. All the outside assistance, not to mention corruption by leading figures, has left Kyrgyzstan with a heavy debt load.

Relations with the Russian Federation

At one time the Kirgiz SSR, highly dependent on Moscow, refined sugar provided from Cuba, while producing some Soviet weapons components. Since independence, the Russian Federation has continued as a close and generally welcome supporter alongside a comparatively liberal and Western-aided government.[30] Poverty and recurrent corruption scandals have contributed to political instability and openness to Russian pressure on a couple of occasions.[31] During the "Tulip Revolution" in 2005, for example, demonstrations forced out physicist Askar Akayev, the country's first president, but when the next president, Kurmanbek Bakiyev, lost Russian support in 2010, he was replaced by another weak President, Almazbek Atambaev, who was more pliant.[32] Perhaps grateful for a $489 million loan settlement with Russia in 2012, Atambaev promised closure of the lucrative American base near Bishkek by 2014.[33] A $200 million debt to Russia was written off two years later. In 2012 an airbase at Kant (near Bishkek), leased by Russia until 2032, was promised $1.5 billion in assistance. According to President Putin, Russia subsidizes the Kyrgyz budget for some $30 million a year. Russia also pays $4.5 million a year for the use of the Karakol testing facility for torpedoes at Lake Issyk-Köl. Russian tourists are a noticeable presence at that famous alpine resort. Oil and gasoline are imported from Russia free of duty, since Kyrgyzstan became a member of the EaEU. A renovated military plant is now operating in Bishkek. Russia also maintains a small communications center and seismic monitoring facility in Kyrgyzstan.

The rubles and dollars earned by the migrants and Russian help allow the purchase of new cars we saw on the streets of Osh, a convincing sign of the luxury consumption by the few wealthy Kyrgyz business people and officials. Nevertheless, the country's foreign debt of over $4 billion (60 percent of its GDP) is worrisome.[34] Clearly all this gives Moscow leverage over Kyrgyzstan's policymakers.

Despite the departure of many former Russian residents, Moscow has various means to maintain security and cultural links. Kyrgyzstan depends entirely for its external security on Russia. The Kant airbase is considered part of the CSTO defense commitment by Kyrgyzstan.[35] Considering Kyrgyzstan's small (ten thousand) armed forces, Russian help could be used for any foreign invasion, however unlikely. About fifteen FSB (Russian secret police) trainees have been sent to Kyrgyzstan, we're told; dozens of Kyrgyz army officers train in Russia every year. Visits by Kyrgyz politicians to Moscow are welcomed.[36] Probably to accommodate migrant workers, there are more flights from Bishkek and Osh to Russia than to any other country.

The "soft power" elements described in Chapter 3 are present in Kyrgyzstan, too, including the Slavic Fund and Russkiy Soyuz and sponsorship of camps and athletic events. In 2015 the widely watched Russian television was given special status. Russian NGOs, such as "Eurasians—New Wave," are available for students.[37] Russian publications are received, but the local press is quite active, too.

Russian efforts to exert "soft power" have not been entirely successful, though, according to interviews by the well-known British specialist David Lewis. Russian officials apparently prefer to work with the authorities rather than to support civil society programs, as Western partners do. Kyrgyzstan's vocal nationalists still bitterly remember Russia's brutal actions in the *Urkun* ("Great Flight") Uprising of 1916, when thousands of native Kyrgyz died or avoided Tsarist enlistment by escaping to China. In 2016 seven politicians were arrested accused of plotting coups.[38] So far, however, Kyrgyz nationalists have little political power, according to our informants.

Relations are not idyllic for this "client state," as some call it. As mentioned before, President Atambaev was unusually frank about economic relations with Russia. According him, Russia's "present economic situation" will not permit it to invest in the Kambarata 1 and 2 dams, nor the Upper Naryn cascade hydroproject owing to unattractive commercial risk for the Russian RAO-UEC energy conglomerate and Uzbekistani opposition.[39] Russia also wanted to construct a new airbase in the Fergana Valley in southern Kyrgyzstan but this was never built, owing to objections from Tashkent, supported by China.[40] On learning of Moscow's displeasure at President Atambaev's expressed view of Russia's financial disability, Atambaev chose a more amenable politician, Sooronbay Jeyenbekov, as prime minister. Jeyenbekov immediately paid Moscow a courtesy call. In the latest presidential election, won by Jeyenbekov in 2017, international observers reported some vote-buying, media bias, and support from the state bureaucracy. For example, as captured on film, a deputy prime minister instructed some civil servants to vote for Jeyenbekov.[41] Once established and constitutionally strengthened in office, in 2018 Jeyenbekov appointed an ally, Mukhamadkaly Abylgazuev to be prime minister. This would seem to indicate what little likely change is forthcoming in Kyrgyzstan's politics—and hence its vulnerability to outside pressures. Now China, a neighbor just to the south, has stepped in to build power lines that will replace lines formerly coming from Uzbekistan and also a thermal power station for more than $300 million.

Kyrgyzstan's accession to the EaEU as of 2014 had to be accepted on Moscow's terms. "No alternative," pleaded then Prime Minister D. Otorbaev.[42] Membership, he explained, would "significantly facilitate" transfer of Kyrgyz labor to the Russian and Kazakhstani markets, as well as crucial remittances, according to former Prime Minister Temir Sariyev.[43] Kyrgyz workers would also receive some social benefits and security for longer stays. On the negative side, however, the country's once lively trade with China is now being affected by EaEU tariffs since Russia has been reinforcing border crossings from China, at an estimated eventual cost of $200 million, starting with the one at Irkeshtam.[44] Kyrgyzstan's massive Dordoi wholesale market near Bishkek fell into deep decline owing to the mandatory tariffs on the consumer goods it always received from China, Turkey, and elsewhere.[45] For example, the duty on men's clothing has been a prohibitive 100 percent! Although a $1 billion Development Fund has been offered by Russia to help restructure the market,[46] business from the EaEU trade doesn't compensate for that. Kazakhstani and Russian re-export customers are fewer owing to their depreciated currencies and recessions.

During 2017 a trade dispute occurred between Kyrgyzstan and its near neighbor Kazakhstan, through which much traffic flows from China. Responding to an accusation that President Nazarbayev was interfering in Kyrgyz internal affairs, Kazakhstan imposed new border controls (in defiance of EaEU rules), causing a huge backup of lorries at the border. Interestingly, Putin refused to intervene. "Moscow does not consider it necessary in a dispute between two neighboring and fraternal countries, believing that its intervention could be perceived negatively by each country," said Russian expert Arkady Dubnov.[47]

As a remote and politically divided country, with poorly developed resources of its own, Kyrgyzstan is not at all likely to present President Putin with obstacles to his main goals. Still, China is playing a growing economic role there, as it is elsewhere in Central Asia, and Russia lacks the material resources to compete.

TAJIKISTAN

Like Kyrgyzstan, the Republic of Tajikistan is also poor and divided north and south. The more than 8 million citizens are mostly Tajik-speaking Sunni Muslims. Despite the emigration of 85 percent of the country's Slavic residents, Russian is taught in schools and is used in business and government. Illicit drugs flow from Afghanistan over the Panj River border. For more than two decades, following a civil war in 1991–1994 with Islamists, tight political control has been in the hands of President Emomali Rakhmon, a former Communist collective farm leader. Islamists are still regarded as the main threat, and many of its activists were arrested or forced to leave.

Economy

Tajikistan's present GDP is $3,200 per capita, earned mostly in agriculture on the five percent of its land that is arable. Reported growth since the 1990s on this low base has been 7 percent yearly. Cotton, the main crop, is exported along with small amounts of minerals. The most important modern industry in Tajikistan is aluminum smelting, using hydropower from the Pamir mountains.[48] Local unemployment is estimated at 10.8 percent.[49] According to our informants in Gorno-Badakhshan's villages along the Afghan border, extreme poverty there is largely neglected by the regime in Dushanbe.[50] Most of the young men are missing from communities there. They work in Russia year-round. Indeed, aside from grants and loans from international sources, a major source of Tajikistan's national income is remittances from Tajik workers employed in Russia (which charges steep fees for documentation, but no visa).

Since Tajikistan has not signed up for the EaEU, in recent years its workers have not had ready access to the Russian labor market, as Kyrgyz do. Russia has required Tajik workers to carry an international passport, an expensive document not previously required. Hundreds of thousands have been barred from entering the Russian Federation. The exact amount of remittances cannot be known. In 2015, a recession year, the number of Tajiks working in Russia fell 13.7 percent, while Kyrgyz numbers hardly changed.[51] Still, at the end of 2016 more than 900,000 Tajiks—or at least 10 percent of its nationals—were reported as working in Russia. In 2017 the migrants' remittances to families in Tajikistan were estimated at $4 billion—half the country's income.[52] In 2018 the amount was still a hefty $2.5 billion, according to the Russian Central Bank's incomplete accounting. [53] This shows the power Russia can exercise through regulating the inflow of laborers from all the poor countries to its south. Tajikistan is the poorest of them all and hence the most vulnerable to Russian pressure.

Despite Rakhmon's self-interested rule, Putin's fear of Islamists and drug suppliers liable to penetrate northwards has allowed the Tajik president to exact aid from Russia on several occasions. The international community has also provided help in dealing with these threats.[54] Debts to Russia have been restructured and energy supplied at reduced cost, though the remaining debt load is heavy. Despite Uzbekistan's objections, Russia is helping build the Sangtuda hydroelectric station—crucial for aluminum development—on the Vakhsh River of Tajikistan and has promised to build three low-capacity hydropower stations to transmit electricity to Afghanistan. But the expensive Rogun Dam project, once promised by Russia, remains unbuilt. During a recent visit, however, Putin held out some twenty projects valued at $33 million, likely to entice Rakhmon to join the EaEU. This strategy has so far failed to work. The Tajik leader is unwilling to jeopardize his country's substantial trade with China.

Relations with the Russian Federation

Tajikistan has only a very small army of its own—about 8,800 active troops—to police its rugged terrain. Because of the ongoing conflict in northern Afghanistan, Russia needs to keep order on the borders of Tajikistan, as well as those of Uzbekistan and Turkmenistan. In 2017 Russia placed Uragan multiple rocket launchers in Tajikistan to counter any possible action of thousands of jihadist militants now thought to be close to the Tajik border. To help supply its long-established 201st airborne mission of some 7,000 troops, Russia has agreed to expand its Ayni airbase near the capital of Dushanbe with a "large quantity" of aircraft. Russia's security interests in protecting against terrorists and drug smugglers do not conflict with those of China, but the presence of Chinese troops in Tajikistan is probably not entirely welcome to Putin. For the same task the United States trains special forces in Tajikistan as well. Moscow might prefer that all these foreign troops remain on the Afghan side of the border.

An instructive example of the challenges Russia encounters doing business in Central Asia is the case of Talco, the Tajik aluminum company that accounts for about 60 percent of that country's exports. Up to 2004, the high point of the Russian-Tajik relationship, the Russian conglomerate Rusal handled Talco trading operations, but in 2006 Rusal was displaced by the Norwegian firm Hydro. The Norwegians agreed to a shady financial arrangement that diverted the fabulous profits from Talco to President Rakhmon and his associates, rather than the Tajik treasury.[55]

Owing to the distance from Russian territory and the predominance of Iranian languages in Tajikistan, Russian media have a weak presence there. In fact RT, Russian television, was denied accreditation, something unheard of elsewhere. Tajikistan's only alternatives are state-controlled.

As we have seen elsewhere in Central Asia, China has assumed an increasing, and quite visible, role in Tajikistan. Tajik consumers buy an increasing share of cheap goods from China, now the country's largest trade partner.[56] Chinese state banks are putting some $150 million into glass and cotton processing plants. A new cement plant brought $100 million, also from China.[57] China has been active in building a road over the mountains to its western province of Xinjang. One condition for that construction aid is the use of Chinese workers by a Chinese company, as we observed there and elsewhere in Central Asia. Aside from this practice and cooperation in stopping Islamists from penetrating the People's Republic's western regions, China seems not to interfere in Tajikistan's internal affairs.

Other countries have some involvement, too. Despite its financial weakness, Iran has participated in financing the Sangtuda-2 hydro station and a key north-south tunnel. Saudi Arabia agreed to contribute $108 million for a highway. Capital goods come in from Germany, a country interested in selling to all the authoritarian regimes of Central Asia. Except for atomic reactors and some arms, Russia is simply not competitive.

Since neither a democratic revolution nor NATO membership are likely to materialize there, Takjistan does not pose the same kind of threat to Putin's Russia that Georgia and Ukraine represent (see Chapter 5). Moscow's main concern in Tajikistan at present is dealing with the drugs that easily penetrate this country's security forces, as well as stopping terrorists who may move north into Russia. With time, China's substantial presence is likely to offer the greatest challenge to Putin's aspiration to maintain Russia's dominant influence in all of the Near Abroad.

TURKMENISTAN

Some 5 million people, nearly all Sunni Muslim by religion, live in Turkmenistan. The country's very large land area (188,000 square miles) is 80 percent covered by the Kara Kum desert. On the east it borders Uzbekistan, as well as Iran and northern Afghanistan to the south. The show-place capital Ashgabat has nearly one million residents. Some Russian is spoken there along with the native Turkoman.

Since the breakup of the USSR Turkmenistan has held to a neutral and mostly isolationist stance. President Gurbanguly Berdymukhamedov succeeded the previous dictator in 2007. He is a kind of sultan with unlimited power and wealth, serving for life under the new constitution. He calls himself Arkadag (the Protector).

Economy

Turkmenistan's per capita income, an estimated $18,100, is earned chiefly by selling its gas and irrigated cotton and grain. Though producing some oil, half for domestic use, Turkmenistan's main export earner has always been its abundant natural gas. The Turkoman are thought to command the world's fourth largest reserves of this valuable resource. At one time its only pipeline went north to Russia, and that gave Gazprom sole control over the price and quantity taken—about 80 billion cubic meters at one time. However, Berdymukhamedov was glad to approve a lucrative Chinese offer to build a gas pipeline all the way to Xinjiang via Uzbekistan and Kazakhstan. This pipeline, opened in late 2009, can carry amounts estimated at 55 billion cubic meters—about five times the current sales to Russia. Despite uneven relations between Turkmenistan and its eastern neighbor, Uzbekistan has allowed a supplementary line which raises the sale of gas to China to 85 billion cubic meters.[58] Turkmenistan also sells a small amount of gas to Iran through two pipelines, but there is a commercial dispute with that country involving an Iranian debt of $2 billion.

Berdymukhamedov has also been trying to interest Turkey and the European Union in Turkmen gas to be supplied via Baku, Azerbaijan. This would require a pipeline under the Caspian Sea, because Turkmenistan has inadequate storage facilities there. The recently signed Caspian Sea Convention would permit Turkmenistan to send its excess gas westward, if it can find some agency or state to build an under-sea pipeline. Russia might want to discourage this unwanted competition by employing naval forces or diplomatic pressure. Another pipeline project from Turkmenistan to Pakistan and India (TAPI) was reportedly begun in 2015 with Asian Development Bank support. It would carry 33 billion cubic meters of gas to the subcontinent at a cost of $10 billion.[59] Of course, that pipeline would have to cross Baluchistan in Afghanistan, and so security would be an issue. Turkmenistan also has Chinese-funded plans for a railroad lines westward from Central Asia to Iran, where China is doing booming business. Berdymukhamedov signed contracts with firms from China, South Korea, and the UAE worth almost $10 billion to develop the very promising South Yolotan fields.[60] Clearly, Russia has found itself outbid for business in this authoritarian state—to China's advantage.

Russia's involvement in the country once included the MTS communications subsidiary, which was required to pay 30 percent of its net profits to Putin's treasury. That relationship has been terminated. The Turkoman now buy most of their consumer goods from Turkey and China.

With lower world prices for his natural gas, Berdymukhamedov has been forced to cut subsidies on utilities, to hold back wages at state-owned firms, and to reduce supplies of staple goods outside of Ashgabat.[61] Sale of dollars was prohibited in early 2016, a sign of distress, and as a result the informal *manat* conversion rate has weakened against the dollar. But since 2018 the government has recovered its income growth and has tried to pay its debts and restore air links to Europe.

Relations with the Russian Federation

Turkmenistan is not a full member of any of Russia's multilateral institutions. It is only an associate member of the CIS and does not allow dual citizenship with outsiders. Though officially neutral, Ashgabat nevertheless served as a transport hub for the United States and NATO supply to their Afghanistan operations. Perhaps more than any other Central Asian country, Turkmenistan has resisted Russian efforts to control its policies and has welcomed trade with and investment from other partners. At the same time, though, its pursuit of neutrality has meant that it has been interested in only a very limited relationship with NATO.

"Black flag" forces—Taliban it seems—have been observed near the border of Turkmenistan.[62] Islamist penetration into this largely desert country would be a problem for Putin, even without any land border with Russia. Though Berdymukhamedov has a large army of 36,500 active troops, any arms supply out of control could enable one or other of the dissatisfied

Turkoman tribes north of the capital to revolt, conceivably in the name of popular democratic rule. The country hardly represents a major success for Russian policy, but its steadfast commitment to neutrality serves to limit the threat it poses.

CONCLUSION

Authoritarian rulers in these five states have repressed democratic dissent, one of Putin's objectives. They were attractive to Western security planners only while Western governments were focused on military operations in Afghanistan. In the economic sphere, these countries are less profitable for Moscow than they were in Soviet times despite their proximity and commercial contacts with Russian-speakers. All of these ex-Soviet Central Asian republics have tried to diversify their trade so as not to rely so heavily on Russia. Kazakhstan, Uzbekistan, and Tajikistan have new links to the outside world, sponsored by the Asian Development Bank's CAREC program. Turkmenistan's ties to China are substantial. The Central Asians send their natural resources and agricultural products—such as cotton, gold, uranium, aluminum, and animal products, as well as oil and gas—to the best world markets, rather than primarily to Russia, though Russia remains a significant customer for ores, fruit, and natural gas. These countries use their export revenues to buy machinery and luxury goods from Western Europe. Hence, Moscow's oligarchs profit rather little from these five new states. They do cooperate with Russia and international agencies such as the UN Health Organization to counter communicable diseases, though drug-taking complicates these efforts. Like Tajikistan and Uzbekistan, Turkmenistan has to guard against an Islamist presence from Afghanistan.

In short, while useful for Putin's goals of combatting terrorism and drug flows, all the authoritarian regimes of Central Asia have been giving priority to their own independence, accumulation of their rulers' wealth, and domestic security, with secondary attention to growth and human welfare, if money becomes available. As is clear from our brief surveys of all of them, Russia has not been able to supply enough money to assist in their development, at least not in comparison with China, and the Chinese have taken advantage of the investment opportunities these states have presented. The West doesn't seem especially interested in their deficient human rights policies, or in developing their energy resources now that prices are low. These authoritarian-led Sunni societies are fairly stable, and as long as their security services do not permit another "color revolution" or other threats to their own or Russia's security, they do not present the kinds of challenges Russia has encountered in the western and southwestern portions of the Near Abroad. These are discussed in Chapters 5 and 6.

NOTES

1. Nicole Contessi, "Foreign and Security Policy Diversification in Eurasia: Issue Splittle, Co-Alignment, and Relational Power," *Problems of Post-Communism*. 62, no. 5 (2015), 299–313.

2. This percentage has steadily fallen owing to the higher birth rates of the Muslim Turkic population, departure of students to study in Russian universities, and outright emigration.

3. The country is in the process of switching Kazakhstani to a Latin alphabet.

4. July 1, 2014.

5. Marlene Laruelle, "Why No Kazakh Novorossiya? Kazakhstan's Russian Minority in a Post-Crimea World," *Problems of Post-Communism* 65, no. 1 (October 24, 2016): 1–14.

6. *The World Almanac* 2019. These are estimates made in 2017–2018, allowing for the cost of living.

7. China holds majority stakes in fifteen companies operating in Kazakhstan's energy sector; more than 30 percent of the crude oil produced in 2010 was already expected to go to China through joint pipelines.

8. *World Bank*, reported in *Financial Times,* January 31, 2018; *www.Republic.ru,* March 28, 2019.

9. Vladimir Paramonov, "Russia's Energy Challenges," *The Journal of International Security Affairs*, 20 (Spring/Summer 2011): 133. Kazakhstan is the world's largest producer of uranium, according to *The Economist*, July 2, 2016.

10. Yevgeny Karasyuk, citing the World Bank's Doing Business report, *www.Republic.ru* , March 20, 2019.

11. *World Almanac 2019.* GDP growth in 2018 was 4 percent.

12. *Financial Times*, September 10, 2016.

13. Andrei Grozin from the CIS Institute, cited in RBC Daily, July 19, 2016. CD 68, no. 29: 13.

14. *The Economist,* June 15, 2019. This kind of criticism was rarely uttered before.

15. *The Economist*, October 20, 2018. Labor leaders have been jailed; press and television are controlled.

16. Roger McDermott, "Kazakhstan Launches Ambitious Military Reform Plan," *Eurasia Daily Monitor*, no. 4 (April 18, 2007).

17. *Interfax KazakhstanOnline*, September 22, 2011.

18. Davinia Hoggarth, "The Role of Islamic Finance: post-colonial market building in Central Asia and Russia." Chatham House online, 2016.

19. Bruno Maçães, *The Dawn of Eurasia* (New Haven, CT:Yale, 2018), 146-47. Kazakhstan owned half this border facility.

20. That amount recovered to $3.9 billion in 2017. Sam Bhutia, "Russian remittances to Central Asia rise again," *Eurasianet.*org. May 23, 2019.

21. "Uzbekistan: Between Russia and the West," *Eurasianet.*org, April 25, 2016.

22. Viktoria Panfilova, *Nezavisimaia Gazeta,* September 2, 2015. CD 67, no. 36: 17.

23. Like all his competitors, Mirziyoyev has a power base in the country. His clan comes from the Dzhizak region, where it controls oil and gas, textile, and banking businesses (one of his allies is Rustam Inoyatov, the Interior Minister, thought to be too old and ill to compete for the top position himself). Erica Marat, "Uzbekistan After Karimov," *Foreign Affairs,* September 7, 2016.

24. Rafael Sattarov, ""Uzbekistan's New Balance of Forces," Carnegie Moscow Center, September 15, 2017.

25. *Financial Times*, February 13, 2018.

26. Aleksandr Pikalov, "Uzbekistan between the great powers: a balance act or multi-vectoral approach," *Central Asian Survey* 33, no.3 (2014): 297–311.

27. Elena Gnedina, "Multi-vector Foreign Policies in Europe: Balancing, Bandwagoning or Bargaining," *Europe- Asia Studies* 67, no. 7 (September 25, 2015): 1007–29.

28. Our informant says another $1–1.5 billion probably comes in informally. These remittances dropped by nearly half in 2015.

29. 7.7 billion rubles a year, of the 100 billion announced by President Putin on a recent trip. Olga Soloyova, *Nezavisimaia Gazeta,* September 18, 2017. CD 69, no.38: 14.

30. David G. Lewis, "Reasserting Hegemony in Central Asia: Russian Policy in Post-2010 Kyrgyzstan," *Comillas Journal of International Relations*, no. 3 (2015): 58-80.

31. For an extensive account, see Martin Spechler, Joachim Ahrens, and Human W. Hoen, *State Capitalism in Eurasia* (Singapore: World Scientific, 2017), Chapter 3.

32. In 2009 President Medvedev approved a $2 billion aid package, some reportedly to go to the president himself. Bakiyev reportedly wanted to renew the Manat airbase and build a military training facility with the Americans in southern Kyrgyzstan. A powerful media campaign and higher energy import prices also hurt Bakiyev's stature. Annette Bohr, "Revolution in Kyrgyzstan—Again," Chatham House, April, 2010, cited in Agnia Grigas, *Beyond Crimea: The New Russian Empire* (New Haven, CT: Yale University Press, 2016), 203. Not accidentally, Medvedev's promised offer was cancelled.

33. Viktoria Panfilova, "Kyrgyzskie kacheli," *Nezavisimaia gazeta*, February 26, 2010. Atambaev, too, has apparently fallen from Russian favor, just before the end of his term.

34. *Eurasianet,* September 29, 2016.

35. www.kg.ru/cis/January 31, 2017. Thanks to Bakhtiyar Ikamberdiyev for this reference.

36. Conversation with Bakhtiyar Ikamberdiyev, Kyrgyz academic, 2017.

37. Lewis,"Reasserting Hegemony in Central Asia," The semi-secret cooperation of policemen is an important element of Central Asian regionalism across official borders, even to China. Alexander Cooley and John Heathershaw, *Dictators without Borders,* (New Haven, Yale, 2017), 185, 204–5.

38. *The Economist*, July 2, 2016.

39. Aleksandr Knyazev, *Nezavisimaia Gazeta ,* January 18, 2016. CD 68, no. 3, 8–9.

40. Stephen Blank, "A Sino-Uzbek Axis in Central Asia?" *Central Asia-Caucasus Analyst,* September 1, 2010.

41. *The Economist*, October 21, 2017, 42.

42. *EurasiaNet,* November 17, 2014.

43. Arkady Dubnov, *Slon.ru.* May 8, 2015, online. CD 67, no.19-20:16. Seriyev was replaced when he failed successfully to complete negotiations with the Canadian gold mining company and was accused of corruption.

44. Mikhail Tishchenko, *Slon.ru*, July 21, 2015. CD 67, no. 30:12.

45. The World Bank estimated the annual turnover in 2012 was some $2.8 billion and re-export of $3.5 billion—a total nearly three-fourths of the country's GDP.

46. Franco Goldini and Elyor Nematov, "Kyrgyzstan: Putin's Eurasia Economic Union and Its Discontents," *The Diplomat*, May 20, 2016. A more recent figure was $200 million for adapting the country to the EaEU, plus a further $500 million for undisclosed projects. *Nezavisimaia Gazeta.,* September 18, 2017.

47. Viktoria Panfilova. *Nezavisimaia Gazeta*, November 30, 2017. CD 69: 48: 16. In mid-2010 the CSTO, which is commanded by Russian officers, refused to intervene in a bloody battle between Kyrgyz and Uzbeks in Osh and Jalalabad, when about two thousand lost their lives.

48. The plant was once partially owned by Rusal—an important Russian investment in the Tajik economy. Martin Spechler, *State Capitalism*, 103.

49. *World Almanac 2019*, 840.

50. Dina R. Spechler, Defne Jones, and Navruz Nekbakhtshoev, "Collective Action for Rural Village Development," *Development* 58, no. 2 (2017). The Aga Khan Foundation supports village development in this mountainous area.

51. Evgeny Vinokurov, *Nezavisimaya Gazeta,* CD 68, no. 31:14. The Central Bank of Russia reported remittances to Tajikistan fell 43 percent in 2015. In response to Russian actions both Kyrgyzstan and Tajikistan were forced to devalue their currencies by 35–42 percent as compared with the 2013. Nate Scheckman, FP, January 22, 2016.

52. "Tajikstan: Feeling the Eurasian Union's gravitational pull," *Eurasianet,* January 31, 2017.

53. "Tajikstan: Rahmon pleads with Putin for amnesty for deported migrants," *Eurasianet.org,* April 18, 2019.

54. Tajikistan's developed security apparatus has regulated the drug trade and yielded "large benefits to senior officials." This source of illicit incomes has largely escaped the central government in neighboring Kyrgyzstan. Lawrence P. Markowitz and Mariya P. Omelicheva, "Disciplined and Undisciplined Repression: Illicit Economies and State Violence in Central Asia's Autocracies," *Post-Soviet Affairs (*July 2018), 11.

55. John Heatherstraw, "Tajikistan amidst globalization: state failure or state transformation?" *Central Asian Survey* 30, no. 1 (March, 2011), 147–68. Apparently some IMF payments went in the same way

56. In 2007 China's share of trade was roughly equal to the Russian's in Tajikistan and Kyrgyzstan. As much of this is petty trade, the benefits go to private shuttle operators (many of them female, in our observation). *IMF Direction of Trade Statistics Quarterly*, June, 2008.

57. Aleksandr Shustov, *Nezavisimaia Gazeta.* May 16, 2016. CD 68, no. 20: 16.

58. *Financial Times*, September 24, 2016.

59. Nicola Contessi, "Is Turkmenistan the Next Central Asian Tiger?" *The Diplomat*, July 15, 2014. There are reported development in tourism, electrical industries, and oil, as well as a new port at Turkmenbashi, but results are yet to be seen.

60. Richard Pomfret, "Exploiting Energy and Mineral Resources in Central Asia, Azerbaijan and Mongolia," *Comparative Economic Studies*, 53 (March, 2011), 20.

61. *The Economist,* February 18, 2017.

62. V. Panfilova, *Nezavisimaia Gazeta,* February 19, 2015, CD 67, no. 8: 19. The Taliban reportedly attacked villages in the east of the country. *The Economist*, July 2, 2016.

Chapter Five

Military Pressure on Southwestern Neighbors

Compared with the Central Asian nations covered in Chapter 4, the five former Soviet states on Russia's southwestern border—Ukraine, Georgia, Moldova, Armenia, and Azerbaijan—are wealthier and closer to Western Europe's attractive democratic and material cultures. All of them have indicated interest in associations offered by the European Union (EU). Among EU members, Poland in particular has welcomed that interest.[1] In view of these countries' locations and histories, such associations pose severe threats to Putin's objectives. They could lead to eventual NATO membership, free trade with Western economies, and liberal democratization. The "Eastern Partnership," inaugurated at the EU summit in 2009, sought both political association and economic integration of all these states and allocated millions of euros to the effort. The EP was correctly seen by many observers as an anti-Russian stance.[2] Since 2014, all five countries have taken part in the EU's "Eastern Neighborhood Policy," which promotes good governance, human rights, economic stabilization, and labor mobility.[3] By now three have visa-free travel rights and trade preferences with the EU.

This common Western orientation has led four of these five countries to seek some kind of regional arrangement among themselves. GUAM, named after its members (Georgia, Ukraine, Azerbaijan, and Moldova), was formed in 1997.[4] Its proclaimed objectives include promoting democratic values, ensuring stable development, enhancing regional security, and participating in European integration. Although it has sought to avoid conflict with Russia, some in Moscow perceive it as a U.S.-backed effort to counter Russian influence in the region.[5] The members share common concerns, which they meet to discuss, but have done little as a group to address the challenges confronting them.

Preventing further pro-Western integration is Putin's chief objective in this southwest region. Active diplomacy on the part of Russia has sought to establish "cooperative" relationships with all these neighbors, with some success. Armenia (as a member) and Moldova (an observer) have accepted EaEU ties, but not Azerbaijan or Ukraine. The Russian president has sometimes used his country's control of energy prices as an inducement or negative pressure, most notably against Ukraine and Georgia. But when his diplomatic efforts have failed, he has resorted to active military means. To see how Russian inducements have fared under Putin's leadership, we must examine each country's demographic and material situation.

UKRAINE

The most important of all the post-Soviet states is Ukraine, a large Slavic nation, long recognized as a separate state by the UN. Its capital, Kyiv, was the earliest center of Russian nationhood. Before World War II, parts of today's Ukraine were Polish territory. Ukrainian, an east Slavic language, is official, but Russian is widely spoken and understood.

Demography

The majority of Ukraine's 44 million people are ethnic Ukrainians. Many are resident on the western, or "right bank," of the Dnipro River. There remain about 17 percent ethnic Russians within Ukraine, especially in the east. About 5–6 million Ukrainian citizens live outside their country, many in Russia or Poland, according to UN data.[6] Emigration has been active since the 1990's because of economic difficulties, clan-based divisive politics, and endemic corruption. Ukraine has enjoyed visa-free entry to the EU since 2017, permitting considerable temporary and permanent location to better employment prospects in Poland and elsewhere. A significantly negative rate of natural increase also contributes to the falling population.

Ukrainian Orthodox Christians are divided between the Kyiv and Moscow Patriarchates, while a number of Greek Catholics and Jews also reside in Ukraine.

Economy

Having failed to recover very much from the deep depression of the 1990s, Ukraine has a per capita GDP of only $8700, a decline of nearly a quarter since 1993. This figure is only one third of Poland's or Russia's today. That reflects Ukraine's severe economic difficulties in recent years, including a loss of much of its metals, machinery, and chemical industries. Ukraine's agricultural and industrial export efforts outside the CIS have not succeeded. [7] Its *hryvna* currency has suffered from high inflation and continual over-valuation. In 2001 and again in 2009, when bills were not paid, Russia cut off the vital natural gas it was piping to Ukraine. Nevertheless, the country has a $2.2 billion defense budget and 202,000 active troops. [8]

Relations with the Russian Federation

Independent Ukraine has long indicated an interest in joining the West, including the EU and NATO. [9] The country has withdrawn from the CIS. In 1994, as part of an agreement with the United States and Russia, its nuclear arsenal was transferred to Russia for destruction. As early as 1995 the Ukrainian government signed a cooperative agreement with NATO. Then in 2002 President Leonid Kuchma declared his nation's intention eventually to join NATO. Even so, during the early years of Putin's administration, Russia agreed to respect the territorial integrity of Ukraine. In 2004 a disputed presidential election marked by massive protests was finally decided in favor of Victor Yushchenko, pro-Western politician closely associated with what was called the "Orange Revolution" that year. Yushchenko's government did poorly, however, and the subsequent parliamentary elections brought pro-Russian Viktor Yanukovych to the prime ministership in 2006. With Putin's open support in the subsequent 2010 presidential election, Yanukovych defeated the pro-European Yulia Tymoshenko. Among the pro-Moscow positions Yanukovych then took was one favoring Russian over the Ukrainian language. His administration also rejected the charge of deliberate genocide perpetrated by Moscow in the Holodomor famine of 1932–1933. Yanukovych also agreed to extend Russia's basing rights at the Black Sea naval base at Sevastopol beyond 2017, leading Russia to announce a modernization and expansion of its military capability there. In return, Kyiv was supposed to obtain a discount from the world price on its natural gas supply from Russia. But this concession was never forthcoming.

This interval of collaboration with Moscow did not last. During the years 2008–2012 Ukraine and the EU were negotiating a free trade and association agreement—a popular orientation for most west-bank Ukrainians, but unwelcome to some easterners and to Moscow. When the EU and Ukraine announced their intention to sign an agreement for a deeper free trade area, anxieties were aroused in Moscow about a possible Western encroachment or threat. It was clear to Putin that in any enhanced trade relationship, such as the EaEU, Ukraine would be vital for success. Before a final agreement, though, the EU failed to offer direct economic aid, and so the Yanokovych government suspended talks with the organization late in 2013. President Putin countered by offering $15 billion over three years and a discount on Russian natural gas deliveries—but also including what amounted to "co-management" of key features of the Ukrainian economy. The notoriously corrupt Yanukovych responded favorably to the Russian offer.[10] Disappointed at the government's failure to reach an agreement with the EU, Ukrainian citizens broke out in violent protests, called "Euromaidan" after the place where they began in central Kyiv. By the next February public pressure—welcomed by the United States and Europe—led the Ukrainian parliament to remove Yanukovych from office. He soon fled.

Denouncing this as a "coup," Putin could not tolerate a possible threat to Russia's security and economic interests. Particularly vulnerable were the large Russian Black Sea fleet at Sevastopol, Crimea, and Putin's hopes for a Eurasian trade bloc. He could easily see that pro-Western parties in the Rada would favor an EU deal instead.

Crimea and the Donbas

Very likely this disorder (and encouragement from Moscow) in 2013 led pro-Russian separatists to rebel in Crimea, a peninsula on the Black Sea whose Russian residents constituted a substantial majority of the population. This territory had been ceded to the Ukrainian SSR by Soviet premier N.S. Khrushchev. Following a hurried referendum policed by Russian troops, the "Republic of Crimea" was returned to Russia in violation of international law and despite the vocal protests of the Western powers. Additional Russian forces reinforced those already in Crimea and also moved up to the border of Ukraine. Even though change of international borders by force had been outlawed by the Helsinki Accords of 1975, NATO did not move. Instead, IMF loans were offered to relieve Ukraine's stressed economy. Significant sanctions on Russian banks were instituted by the United States and the EU, preventing long-term energy deals in the Federation. China and other post-Soviet independent states did not recognize the border changes either.

A similar takeover in April of that year by pro-Russian activists brought Russian soldiers in unmarked uniforms and heavy equipment to the southeastern Ukrainian provinces of Donetsk and Luhansk (the Donbas). Over the next three years, thousands died in the fighting and 450,000 refugees fled, mostly to Russian territory. An estimated 1.6 million were internally displaced, according to the UN High Commissioner on Refugees. By 2018 pro-Russian separatists still controlled the region by means of the infiltrated hybrid force, together with cyber-warfare, propaganda, and economic blackmail.[11] Although the Ukrainian and ethnic Russian separatists in the two provinces proclaimed their desire to join the Russian Federation, Putin did not comply, perhaps owing to the likely costs of energy, public sector salaries, and food aid, as experienced in Crimea.[12] These people will be able to obtain Russian passports, however.[13] With the Kyiv government weakened to near economic collapse—national income fell some 16 percent over 2014–2015—Putin was able to impose an armistice, embodied in the Minsk Protocol, that reduced, but failed to end, violence along the cease-fire line in 2014. The 2015 "Minsk II Agreement," negotiated with the help of German Chancellor Angela Merkel and French President François Hollande, envisioned enhanced local self-government in the rebellious eastern regions and did not make peace in the Donbas contingent on the return of Crimea to Ukraine.[14] None of the parties were satisfied with the terms of this second agreement, and it, too, has failed to halt the violence. In the four years that have followed with episodes of fighting and truce, the entry of OSCE peacekeepers has not changed the situation. Facing a rebuilt Ukrainian army are an estimated five thousand hybrid-Russian soldiers stationed there at substantial cost to the Kremlin. The two Donbas provinces retain their own militias and administrations.[15] Ex-president Pyotr Poroshenko was unsuccessful in his efforts to punish Russia for its "aggression." The new President, Volodomyr Zelensky, promises better relations with the Russian Federation. If new elections increase the political strength of pro-Russian parties in the Rada—a shift that would reduce the threat of Westernization of Ukraine—Putin could perhaps agree to terminate the unofficial and expensive occupation of Donetsk and Lugansk.

Though paying a high international political and financial price for preventing dismembered Ukraine from joining NATO—utility bills to the two regions remain unpaid[16] and normal commerce disrupted[17]—Putin has successfully achieved his goals in this vital part of the "new abroad": no foreign forces (other than Russian), no economic integration with the EU, and a docile population and regime anxious to avoid overt conflict with Moscow. According to *The Economist,* "in many ways, Donetsk and Luhansk are now more integrated into Russia than Ukraine. Commerce is carried out in rubles. Schools have moved to Russian international standards. . . . Russia has begun accepting passports from the unrecognized republics when people buy train and plane tickets." Putin says that, after all, Russia and Ukraine are "one people." Russian representatives assert that the situation has become more peaceful, with normal entry and exit from the area. With Russian-speakers exposed to intense propaganda from Russian television, it's not surprising that many left-bankers favor membership in the EaEU along with Russia, rather than the European Union, which is strongly favored by right-bank Ukrainians.

Still, Putin cannot claim complete success. Overall, Ukraine's bilateral trade with Russia was down 30 percent in 2016.[18] Russian nationalists, who generally take pride in Russia's international status, nevertheless complain about the damage to houses and property in Donbas.[19] If quiescent, right-bankers still bitterly resent and vocally denounce Russian occupation.[20] In a highly publicized symbolic move with Kyiv's support, the Orthodox Church of Ukraine with its seven thousand parishes has been declared independent of the larger Moscow patriarchy by the Constantinople authorities. Pro-EU parties have strengthened their majority in the Rada. Ukraine's military strength has recovered, even if its GDP has been slow to do so. Although Ukraine now must pay three to four times the (albeit lower) price for natural gas than it once did and major new foreign investments are not coming in,[21] by 2017 Ukraine was slowly reviving and was able to get debt relief (a 20 percent "haircut") from the outside world—except from creditor Russia. By September 2017 Ukraine could float a $3 billion IMF bond in world financial markets, though at an expensive rate of 7.3 percent.[22] Thus Russia does not command the leverage over Ukrainian policies that he would like to have.

Top European foreign ministers have discussed putting a peacekeeping force between the two combatant sides and removing mines. Truncated as it is at present, Ukraine has been trying to attract more European assistance and political backing by proposing various projects with GUAM members Georgia, Azerbaijan, and Moldova, including free trade. But finance for these schemes is mostly lacking.[23] Ukraine has received more than $350 million in aid from the United States, as well as an $80 million shipment of anthracite coal, in an effort to reduce dependence on Russian fuels.[24] Having a significantly reduced trade with Russia, Ukraine is trying to shift it to the EU and China.[25] The government is introducing new travel restrictions for Russian citizens, and is reportedly working to meet NATO standards for its weapons. A Constitutional provision calls for full membership in NATO and the EU. However, Putin's greatest fears are unlikely to be realized anytime soon. No one in Ukraine expects any bid to join NATO will succeed in the foreseeable future. As the diplomatic NATO Secretary General Jens Stoltenberg says, that "depends on reforms."

GEORGIA

This medium-sized state is separated from the Russian Federation by the Caucasus mountains. The breakaway regions of Abkhazia and South Ossetia, which have separate languages, are recognized as independent by Russia, but few other countries. About 18 percent of Georgia's territory is not under control from its capital, Tbilisi. With a population of about 5 million, mostly Orthodox Christians, Georgia has lost considerable population from this loss of territory and emigration.

Economy

Famed for its fruits and wine, Georgia also produces steel, machine tools, and electrical appliances. Its GDP per capita is $10,700. Having suffered a deep depression in the 1990s, the country has now recovered production but still suffers over 11 percent unemployment. The government of President Giorgi Margvelashvili and then-Prime Minister Giorgi Kvirkashvili, was able in 2014–2015 to address Georgia's financial weakness by floating the *lari* currency, keeping the interest rate at 7.5 percent and inflation low to manage Georgia's public debt, and achieving moderate growth. Georgia's new female president Salome Zourabachvili comes from the Georgia Dream Party, which is led by the idiosyncratic billionaire Bidzina Ivanishvili. The Georgia Dream party remains somewhat indefinite about the country's future but wants to "normalize" relations with Russia.[26] Georgia is rated "partly free" by Freedom House and has achieved a decent rating (46 out of 180) by Transparency International for its efforts to deal with corruption.

Like Ukraine, Georgia is interested in a closer functional relationship with the EU even if it must remain short of membership. Its ruling coalition

Party signed an economic cooperation and trade agreement with the EU, including visa-free travel there. The EU's "four unions" are the format for this integration: the Customs Union, Energy Union, Digital Single Market, and the Schengen area. The effort to incorporate Georgia into these arrangements will test the patience and resources of Brussels.

Relations with the Russian Federation

After Georgia's declaration of independence in 1991, former Soviet Foreign Minister Eduard Shevardnadze served as president through several coup attempts before being unseated by massive protests. Under his leadership Georgia joined the CIS and accepted three Russian bases. In return Putin had the small region of Adzharia returned from a rebellious warlord to Georgia proper.[27] Shevardnadze was replaced by pro-American Mikhail Saakashvili as a result of the "Rose Revolution" in 2003. The new president introduced liberal anti-corruption measures with modest, though energetically proclaimed, success. The American Administration under George W. Bush, who saw Georgia as a "beacon of democracy" for the region, raised the possibility of NATO membership at a meeting in Bucharest in 2008. Saakashvili also proclaimed his desire to join NATO, something unacceptable to Moscow. He seemed to enjoy provoking Putin, whom he reportedly called "Lilli-Putin."[28]

In an attempt to ensure its independence from Russia, Georgia increased its military budget by some ten times from its 2004 level to 2008, until it constituted a full 5 percent of its GDP. Russia countered with a trade ban and was prepared for war by 2008. When in August of that year ethnic Georgians in the north of the country came under fire from Russia's local Ossetian allies, the impetuous Saakashvili attacked first into South Ossetia.[29] Russian forces responded by moving into Georgian territory in a rehearsed five-day campaign supported by a cyber-attack

Ever since then, Russian troops have occupied land within Georgia proper in violation of the Cease-fire Agreement negotiated by the EU. Furthermore, the Russians have continued to build up army bases in both Abkhazia and South Ossetia and have supported the breakaway enclaves with cooperation and military agreements, citizenship and passport offers, and welfare payments. South Ossetia (capital Tskhinvali) has given Russia control over its customs and defense in exchange for a subsidy estimated at $89 million[30] for its small number of citizens, but Abkhazia (capital Sokhumi) seems to want to preserve semi-independence.[31] Ethnic Georgians have been pushed out of these areas, and OSCE and UN monitoring missions have been prevented from entering. An EU Monitoring Group patrols the borders. Besides the occupation of these enclaves, Russia boycotted Georgia's exports, but when Saakashvili lost to the Georgia Dream in parliamentary elections and in the subsequent presidency in 2013, Russia removed its trade embargo and visit restrictions. Along with Turkey and Azerbaijan, Russia is now a major trade partner. According to Georgi Menabde, there are several pro-Russian NGOs operating in Georgia.[32]

Europe and the United States have done little to counter these secessions except to send some economic aid and facilitate the construction of a NATO training center in 2015. A Deep and Comprehensive Free Trade Area now eases Georgia's still modest visa-free trade with the EU. A deep water port at Anaklia on the Black Sea, now under construction, will offer importers routes around Russia for most goods. To a great extent, then, military force has solved Putin's problem with Georgia. Not an immediate candidate for NATO, owing to its uncertain borders, Georgia voluntarily supplies troops to the NATO mission in Afghanistan and joins in NATO exercises and sanctions. Former Prime Minister Kvirkashvili was quoted as seeing this as a "step" to NATO membership, if the "frozen conflict" over Abkhazia and South Ossetia could be resolved peacefully. Georgia has been seen as the "strategic underbelly" of the Western alliance. But given this leadership and its goals, a repetition of the "Rose Revolution" seems unlikely.

ARMENIA

The small mountainous Republic of Armenia borders Georgia, Azerbaijan, and Turkey. Russia is thirty miles to northeast. This country has attracted more attention than most of comparable size because of its historical extent (including part of present-day Turkey and Iran) and its many compatriots living abroad, especially in the United States and Russia. Armenian ex-patriots and descendants live in other CIS countries, too,[33] and involve themselves in NGOs in their former country—for example, in publicizing the 1915 genocide in Turkey.

Demography

This smallest CIS member country has only three million inhabitants, nearly all Armenian Apostolic Christians. Russian language familiarity is common, though the government has refused official status for it. Perhaps 10 percent of the population hold Russian passports, useful for business trips. An estimated one and a half million Armenians have left the country since 1990, most of them emigrating to Russia.

Just prior to the disbanding of the USSR in 1991, the heavily-Armenian population of the mountainous area of Nagorno-Karabakh seceded from the Azerbaijan SSR. Then in 1992–1994 Armenia fought a very costly war with Azerbaijan, resulting in Armenian occupation of that enclave. Veterans from Nagorno-Karabakh conflict remain a powerful bloc in Armenia's politics today.[34] Voters in Nagorno-Karabakh adopted a pro-independence constitution in 2006, a move the EU rejected.

Economy

Armenia is fairly well-off, with a GDP per capital of $9500 as of 2018. It has a low tax rate, a stable *dram* currency, a good business climate, and an expansive informal sector, all contributing to decent growth of about 6–7 percent yearly since 2000. Diamond processing, machine-building, and its export of wines and valuable minerals all contribute to the economy. Even so, the unemployment rate is a disturbing 18.2 percent, contributing to sizable migration. Armenia's largest single trade and investment partner is now Russia.

Relations with the Russian Federation

Russia controls Armenia's electrical grid, its gas supply, and its railroads—a very well-known fact in the country. In 2015 demonstrations against electric rate increases by a Russian-owned utility led to a take-over by a local group—and reversal of the price decisions.

Putin has been backing Armenia in its continuing tension with neighboring Azerbaijan over the issue of Nagorno-Karabakh. Armed clashes resumed in 2015–2016, which Russia entered to broker. Owing to this abiding enmity and a long quarrel with Turkey, Armenia is surrounded on three sides by hostile powers. Russia, its closest ally, is separated from Armenia by Georgia, and that country might resist any attempt by Moscow to send troops through its territory. This situation generates a strong sense of vulnerability in the government and the population at large. The well-equipped Russian base at Gyumri, adjacent to the Turkish border, is therefore considered vital for security, as are good relations with Russia.

Armenia once considered signing an Association Agreement with the EU, but a variety of pressures—economic and military—upon President Serzh Sargsyan's government forced it to cancel these plans and enter the EaEU in 2015, despite considerable domestic opposition.[35] Armenia is also a member of the CSTO and cooperates with its allies on air defense. A new bilateral defense treaty, signed in 2016, commits Russia to defend Armenia from an Azerbaijani attack, provides more arms against that possibility, and extends the lease on the Gyumri base for another three decades.[36] With a rather large army of 44,000 and a $428 million defense budget, together with Russian aid, Armenia will not be easy to dislodge from its conquests. Notably, though, Armenia did supply NATO troops for Afghanistan, Iraq, and Kosovo operations.[37]

Russia did not intervene in Armenia's 2018 parliamentary elections, which were contended in the capital Yerevan over issues of corruption. They resulted in the appointment of Nikol Pashinian as prime minister, a post with increased constitutional powers.[38] He asserts a "multi-vector" foreign policy—not a "color revolution, says Pashinian.[39] The new government is committed to fighting corruption, reducing the shadow economy, and developing IT, tourism, and its agricultural specialties (grapes). Armenia has renegotiated a Comprehensive and Enhanced Partnership Agreement with the EU which provides financial and technical assistance and "one of the few available ways to offset some of Russia's pressure."[40] Armenia abstained from European Neighborhood members' condemnation of the Crimean takeover.[41]

Even with all these developments from Pashinian's "velvet revolution," Armenia remains tied to Russia. A kind of unstated protectorate, Armenia can be no threat to Putin's ambitions or plans. In fact, along with Kazakhstan and Tajikistan, Armenia is one of the Russian president's most reliable and least problematic allies.

AZERBAIJAN

The independent Republic of Azerbaijan borders the Russian Federation over the Caucasus Mountains, as well as Georgia to the north and the Caspian Sea and Iran (with its sizable Azeri minority) to its south. Once a Turkish province, Azerbaijan was conquered by Tsarist Russia at the beginning of the nineteenth century. A considerable portion of Azerbaijan (Nagorno-Karabakh) is occupied by Armenian forces, as mentioned above.

Demography

With over 10 million people, Azerbaijan is an authoritarian Muslim-majority state, like those of Central Asia.[42] Because of the war with Armenia, there are many Azeri refugees from Nagorno-Karabakh, together with some 170,000 Armenians, among the 2.2 million residents of the capital, Baku. Like the other Muslim-majority republics in the Near Abroad, Azerbaijan has experienced a considerable population increase (33.6 percent) since 1992. Energy-rich Azerbaijan enjoys a GDP of $17,500 per capita.

President Ilham Aliyev[43] wants to make his country a railway transit hub for both India and Russia. Lines would go from Mumbai to Baku, on to Kars, Turkey, then through to the Balkans or Moscow. Azerbaijan would thus be part of China's new Silk Road. The ambitious government is also exploring new energy routes through Georgia and Turkey. The Caspian Sea Convention signed by the five littoral states on August 12, 2018, when ratified, could allow construction of a natural gas pipeline from Turkmenistan (or Kazakhstan) to Azerbaijan. By supplying ultimate customers in Turkey or Europe, any pipeline would be profitable for Azerbaijan, as well as for Chinese or Western investors.

Economy

With its long-established energy resources, Azerbaijan is a relatively wealthy country. It has benefitted from oil and gas pipelines through Georgia to Turkey. After the energy recession of 2014–2015 its *manat* currency was devalued. With new growth, Azerbaijan's poverty rate has reportedly been reduced from 50 percent in 2000 to only 5 percent these days, with wages and pensions up seven to eight times over fifteen years. A new agreement with BP, Chevron, Statoil and other energy giants promises new technologies and investments with a 75 percent cut to go to the State Oil Company of the Azerbaijanian Republic. The EBRD has invested $500 million for a new gas pipeline.[44] Luxury apartment and hotel construction in Baku for the 2015 European Games have been noticeable. Tourism, especially from the more religious Middle East states, is booming. Thus prosperity seems assured for the future.

With good relations and sizeable investments from Turkey, Georgia, the United States, and rich Azeris resident in Moscow, the autocratic Aliyev regime has few dangerous external enemies. Internally, though, deteriorating human rights are source of constant unrest and pressure on the government.[45]

In response Aliyev has increased repression of political opponents and shut down independent media, ignoring Council of Europe criticism. Freedom House rates Azerbaijan "not free." Newly re-elected (by 86 percent) for a seven- year term until 2025, Aliyev is supported by a new cabinet of technocrats and the appointment of his wife, Mekhriban Pashayeva, who comes from an influential clan, to be vice president. No color revolution seems likely here, a reassuring fact for Putin.

Relations with the Russian Federation

To take off-shore Caspian gas to Turkish markets Moscow has agreed with Baku to use of the seabed. Azerbaijan's existing contacts with Western customers (for instance, via the Baku-Ceyhan pipeline) may be annoying to Putin, but Azerbaijan is still too small an energy competitor and too remote to pose a problem for him.

Publicly Putin continues to work for a solution of the Nagorno-Karabakh issue with the Azerbaijanis on acceptable terms. Not long ago, in 2016, small incidents with Armenians occurred on the border of the Naxçivan enclave, and Putin promptly offered mediation. President Aliyev recently bought some $4 billion of Russian arms, maybe in the hope that Russia will be neutral in any future conflict with Armenia. The naval arms Azerbaijan is buying from NATO sources and the Israelis may also create problems for Armenia in the future, if Russia doesn't intervene. Azerbaijan's government allocates $1.4 billion in its defense budget to support a sizeable army of 66,950. So Aliyev can continue to talk tough about Armenia's occupation of disputed territories, fully aware of Armenia's patron in Moscow. This "frozen conflict" makes Azerbaijan unattractive for membership in the NATO or the EU. Baku has joined a number of regional groupings, including the European Network, but none seems effective.[46] Putin can concentrate his attention elsewhere.

MOLDOVA

The Republic of Moldova is a small, land-locked nation separated from the Black Sea by Ukrainian territory. Before World War II it was part of Romania. Moldova declared independence from the USSR in 1991 but ever since the 1990s, it has been divided by the Dniester River from the occupied Transdnistria region. The larger western part of Moldova (capital Chişinău) was once the former Romanian province of Bessarabia, but in a plebiscite Moldovan voters declined to reunite with Romania. The smaller eastern district of Transdnistria (capital Tiraspol) has many more ethnic Russians and Ukrainians than Moldovans. The country has no border with the Russian Federation, but Russian platoons are stationed in Transdnistria on rotations. Schools and official meetings there are conducted in Russian.

Demography

Most of the 3.5 million citizens of Moldova are Orthodox Christian and speak a language nearly identical to Romanian written in Latin script, although Russian and Ukrainian languages are also heard. There is also a small Gagauz minority. Despite a positive rate of natural increase, the population is falling owing to emigration, mostly to the Russian Federation. Some Moldovans have Romanian passports, facilitating trade westward, even with goods from Transdnistria.

Economy

A predominantly agricultural country, Moldova has a per capita GDP of only $5700, based on export sales of sugar and vegetable oil, mostly westward. Growth has been only two percent yearly, and reported unemployment is about five percent. Imports, especially energy, come from Gazprom, along with other items from Romania and Ukraine. The country's banks have Russian connections, allegedly involved in money laundering. A banking scandal troubled the country in the early 2010s. Nonetheless, since 2010 Moldova has received 300–400 euro annually from the EU and other Western sources.[47] NGO regulations like Russia's are being "considered." After a meeting with Putin in January 2019, Moldova was granted a six month relief from import duties on its fruits, vegetables, canned goods, and wine.[48] Thus, Moldova's material interests are split east and west.

Relations with the Russian Federation

At present Moldova is likewise divided in its allegiance and apparent political direction between east and west. At one time the independent Moldovan government took a pro-EU position and hoped for economic assistance from Romania, which has been a member of NATO since 2004. Moldova signed an association agreement with the EU in 2014 and initiated public administration reforms that organization urged. Since Russia has insisted on non-aligned status for Moldova, this action prompted objection from Foreign Minister Lavrov,[49] and resulted in a Russian ban on Moldovan wines and mineral water. Up to recently a parliamentary coalition of Prime Minister Pavel Filip backed by the oligarch Vladimir Plahotniuc, has been pro-European. This pair reportedly hopes outside influences on the electorate will play a stronger pro-Western role.[50] Moldova quietly cooperates with NATO, too.[51]

On the other side, the Orthodox Metropolitan usually favors the pro-Russian parties. Television (*Perviy Kanal*) and newspapers come from Russia. In 2016 Moldovan citizens elected Igor Dodon as President after a banking scandal. A Socialist politician, he wanted a partnership with Russia and integration with the EaEU and said he would accept Russian peacekeepers, but without cancelling the country's association with the EU—or presumably giving up Western money, either![52] Later Dodon opposed any trade deal with the EU.[53] Then-Prime Minister Filip countered that this would be beyond the president's legal powers.[54] A new government headed by Prime Minister Maia Sandu, a former World Bank official, was elected in 2019. She represents a coalition of the pro-Russian party and the pro-Western New Platform.[55] Filip has disputed the results. Amidst these arguments and ideological divisions, the country is nevertheless rated "partly free" by Freedom House.

In 2006 voters in Transdniester strongly supported independence from (western) Moldova and eventual union with Russia. This "frozen conflict" has long been seen as a means for Moscow to exert pressure on independent politicians.[56] Moeover, the unresolved border with Russian-armed, disorderly Transdnistria would slow any NATO expansion in the area.[57] Considering the divided loyalties and interests, whatever worries impecunious Moldova ever posed to Putin's goals from distant Moscow's vantage point need not occupy him these days. Moldova's eastern neighbor is of far greater concern to the Russian President.

CONCLUSION

In sum Russia's military involvement in these five states, even when inactive, poses a barrier to any but peaceful and largely financial Western involvement in their affairs. There doesn't appear to be much Western interest in dealing with the "frozen conflicts" which affect them all, thus justifying

Russian diplomatic involvement as needed. Putin's Russia has paid a very high price, in the form of sanctions and diplomatic isolation, for its assertive policies in Ukraine. From the vantage point of the President, however, there is no doubt that these policies have helped immeasurably in his quest to maintain Russia's dominance in the Near Abroad and thereby ensure its great power status.

NOTES

1. Marlene Laruelle and Jean Radvanyi, *Understanding Russia* (Lanham, MD: Rowman & Littlefield, 2018), 105.

2. U.S. ambassador to Warsaw Victor Ashe wrote in a dispatch to Washington, "The Eastern Partnership and other Polish policies in the region aim to counter a resurgent Russia . . . and to spur the reforms needed for eventual EU membership and stem growing Russian influence." A Wikileaks cable of December 12, 2008, quoted by Justyna Zając, *Poland's Security Policy* (London: Palgrave Macmillan, 2016), 128.

3. These five have also signed Protocols with the EU. The EU gave €15 billion to the ENP countries in 2014–2020 on a competitive basis. As revised in 2015 the ENP does not include "irregular" migration. Belarus is also an ENP member and will be discussed in Chapter 6. ENP does not promise EU membership at any future time.

4. Armenia, Russia's closest ally among the five, has avoided association with GUAM. Uzbekistan joined in 1999 but withdrew in 2005 when the other members refused to condone its massacre of protestors in Andijan earlier that year.

5. "Axis of Evil Shaping against Moscow," *Kommersant*, March 3, 2005.

6. *The New York Times*, June 15, 2018. Data refer to 1990 and 2007.

7. Ukraine's export potential into the EU was always questionable because its manufactured products are often low-quality and its abundant grain would face the EU's protective Common Agricultural Policy.

8. *World Almanac 2018*, 845.

9. Sergei Zhiltsov, *Nezavisimaia Gazeta,* April 23, 2018: 11. Both former President Petro Poroshenko and the Rada parliament approved this objective and disallowed dual citizenship.

10. James Sherr, "Ukraine: Door Closed?" in S. Frederick Starr and Svante Cornell, eds., *Putin's Grand Strategy: The Eurasian Union and its Discontents.* (Washington, D.C.: Central Asia-Caucasus Institute and Silk Road Studies Program, 2014), 122–23.

11. *The Economist,* January 27, 2018.

12. Sergey Aleksashenko, a former Russian banker, estimates that Moscow has spent $2.3 billion on Crimea since 2014, including a highway from the new Kerch bridge to Sevastopol and a new airport. *The Economist,* June 8, 2019. This amounts to three years of national healthcare services.

13. Neil Macfarquhar, "Outrage Grows as Russia Grants Passports to Ukraine's Breakaway Regions," *The New York Times*, April 26, 2019.

14. Zając, 167.

15. *The Economist,* February 11, 2017.

16. Yuri M. Zhukov, "Trading hard hats for combat helmets: The economics of rebellion in eastern Ukraine," *Journal of Comparative Economics* 44 (no. 1): 1–15.

17. S. Zhiltsov, *Nezavisimaia Gazeta.,* April 21, 2017; CD 69, no.17: 15–16.

18. *Vedomosti*, July 26, 2017. CD 69, no. 30: 14.

19. Pal Kosto, "Crimea vs. Donbas: How Putin Won Russian Nationalist Support—and Lost It Again," *Slavic Review* 75 (no. 3), 702–25.

20. *The Economist,* February 18, 2017. Opinion in the "right (western) bank" is more pro-European, while the citizens father to the south and east are more mixed and pro-Russian.

21. Yevgeniya Albats, *New Times,* December 4, 2018, quoting EBRD Chief Economist Sergei Guriev.

22. As a condition for this loan, the government had to agree to higher energy prices. The EBRD has put in place a five-year plan for economic recovery. CD 70, no. 49 (2018): 18.

23. Zhiltsov, 11.

24. Center on Global Interests, Daily Russia Brief, September 13, 2017. Defensive missiles may be forthcoming.

25. Oxford Analytica, cited in "Ukraine reaps benefits of trade deal with EU," *Financial Times,* September 11, 2018.

26. Sergei Mardenonov, *Vedomosti*, August 3, 2018. CD 70, no. 31: 10.

27. Robert Donaldson and Vidya Nadkarni, *The Foreign Policy of Russia,* 6th ed. (Routledge, 2019), 207.

28. *The Economist*, January 13, 2018.

29. According to the Tagliavini Report for the Council of the European Union, "Independent international fact-finding mission on the conflict in Georgia," III, 2009. www.ceiig.ch/Report.html.

30. L. Bershidsky, *Bloomberg,* November 13, 2018, in *Russia Matters*, November 12, 2018.

31. Agnia Grigas, *Beyond Crimea: The New Russian Empire* (New Haven, CT: Yale University Press, 2016), 134.

32. Grigas, 224.

33. Georgia, Ukraine, and Uzbekistan contain the largest numbers.

34. Lawrence Boers, "The South Caucasus: Fracture without End?" in Anna Ohanyan, ed. *Russia Abroad: Driving Regional Fracture in Post-Communist Eurasia and Beyond.* (Washington, D.C: Georgetown University Press, 2018), 97.

35. Armen Gregoryan, "Armenia: Joining under the Gun," in S. Frederick Starr and S. Cornell eds., *Putin's Grand Strategy: the Eurasian Union and its Discontents.* (Washington, D.C.: Central Asia-Caucasus Institute and Silk Road Studies Program, 2014), 98–109.

36. F. Ismailzade, "Russian Arms to Armenia Could Change Azerbaijan's Foreign Policy Orientation," *Central Asia-Caucasus Analyst* 11, no. 2 (January 28, 2009). Since Armenia does not border any other EaEU country it had to ask for numerous exceptions to EaEU rules.

37. Grigas, 221.

38. Recently Robert Kocharyan, former president of Armenia (and friend of Putin's) and Yuri Khachaturov, former CSTO secretary-general and commander of the Yerevan garrison, were jailed on charges stemming from his participation in a violent rally in 2008 in which Pashinian participated.

39. Arnold Khachaturov, "in *Novaya Gazeta*, August 18, 2018. CD 70, no. 32: 14–15.

40. Andriy Tyushka, "Seeking the Eastern Partnership's greatest integer," *New Eastern Europe*, March–April (no. 2), 89. Tyushka is a research fellow on the ENP at the College of Europe, Warsaw.

41. While most of the CIS countries condemned Russia's annexation of Crimea or remained silent on the issue, Armenia enthusiastically endorsed the referendum Moscow held there, calling it an example of "the realization of the people's right to self-determination." Yerevan has promoted that principle in its conflict with Azerbaijan. The government may have hoped that the Crimean precedent would bolster its case for the legitimacy of its occupation of

Nagorno-Karabakh. "Armenia Sides with Russia over Crimea," *Economist,* March 25, 2014. At the very least, Armenia's stand helped to strengthen that country's relationship with Russia.

42. In contrast with the rest of the Former Soviet Union, most of Azerbaijan's Muslims are Shiites, like those who live in neighboring Iran.

43. Son of the first leader of independent Azerbaijan, Gaidar Aliyev, a pro-Russian Communist, who died in 2003. Ilham once taught at the Moscow State Institute of International Relations.

44. Neil Buckley and Henry Foy, "EBRD to lend $500 m. for Azerbaijan pipeline," *Financial Times*, October 18, 2017.

45. Vakhtan Dzhanashia, "Azerbaijan at a Crossroads," *Ekspert,* April 16, 2018 condensed in CD 70, no.16: 14. Though suffering from displacements, he writes, the Kurdish elite wishes to preserve its friendship with Armenia against the Turks.

46. Lawrence Boers, "The South Caucasus: Fracture without End?" in Ohanyan, Chapter 4.

47. Andrey Devyatkov, "Dynamics of Russian Power in Moldova," Foreign Policy Research Institute, March 22, 2017.

48. Vladimir Solovyov, *Kommersant,* January 9, 2019.

49. Vesti TV 2014, cited in Robert Nalbandov, "From Donbas to Damascus," in Ohanyan, 48.

50. *Nezavisimaia gazeta* (by Svetlova Gamova), March 27, 2017. CD 69, no.: 13: 14.

51. Angela Stent, *Putin's World* (New York: Twelve, 2019), 159.

52. *Izvestia*, November 15, *2016.* CD 68, no. 46: 14–15.

53. "In Russia, Moldovan President Says He May Scrap EU Trade Pact," Reuters, January 17, 2017.

54. Fox News, January 18, 2017.

55. *The New York Times,* June 15, 2019.

56. Laruelle and Radvanyi, 98.

57. Grigas, *Beyond Crimea*, 107. This also applies, she says, to Georgia and Ukraine.

Chapter Six

Resisting NATO Pressure: Northwest Border States

Any direct military threat from NATO upon the Russian Federation would probably come from the states bordering the St. Petersburg region and the Baltic Sea. Putin's efforts to counter that potential threat have greatly involved CIS member Belarus. Those efforts have increasingly been directed against NATO members Estonia, Latvia, and Lithuania, all of which have borders with Russia. Moscow's policy toward Finland, a non-member which cooperates with NATO defenses, has emphasized the maintenance of a "normal" relationship that aims at avoiding any incentive for that hitherto neutral country to join this hostile alliance.

BELARUS

Never an independent political entity, the Belorussian SSR was nevertheless made an independent member of the United Nations at Stalin's demand. Today the Republic of Belarus remains a separate state within the CIS with its capital in Minsk. Despite the many expressed intentions on both sides from the late 1990s to unite it with Russia,[1] Putin would merely say that this "Union Treaty" would take years and would remain on paper for the foreseeable future.[2] Only some unifying legal arrangements for housing and jobs have been completed. According to Prime Minister Medvedev, union would require identical taxes, prices, and tariff rates.

Demography

Undoubtedly the nine million people of Belarus have the closest ethnic and linguistic ties to Russia among all CIS members. Russian is an official language and is spoken widely, along with the related east Slavic Belarusian. Russian-language media (and its pro-Putin messages) easily penetrate the Belarusian broadcast area, perhaps accounting for the Belarusian public's acquiescence in the Crimean take-over and other initiatives of Putin's. While dual citizenship is not allowed, intermarriage with Russians is fairly common. Many Belarusians work within Russia, too. Some 15,000–20,000 Belarusians study at Russian universities. With this easy access and familiarity, however, only five percent of the Belarusian population wants union with Russia at present, fewer than expressed this desire in previous local surveys. Belarus lost about seven percent of its population from 1992 to 2017, probably owing to its low birth rate and emigration.[3]

Economy

As it did in Soviet times, Belarus produces tractors, metal-cutting tools, peat, timber, potash, potatoes, flax, and milk on its hilly and marshy lowlands. Among the reasons for Putin's reluctance to go ahead with a political union have probably been the unreformed state-run economy in Belarus, which needs sizable energy subsidies and help in cleaning up from and otherwise dealing with the tremendous impact of the 1986 Chernobyl nuclear accident in nearby Ukraine.[4] The country has a GDP per capita of $18,900, a third less than Russia's. It has suffered negative growth lately, and unemployment of more than 11 percent.[5] But alongside the faltering state enterprises has grown up a private sector, now some half of the economy.[6]

About 86 percent of Belarusians' inter-union transactions are with Russia. As Belarus is a member of the EaEU, there are normally no customs barriers to goods flowing to or from Russia. The Minsk government has proposed unifying its independent ruble currency with the Russian one. This proposal has been turned down, probably for fear of misuse. After all, Belarus has an inflation rate of 11.8 percent, much higher than Russia's. This difference would lead to sharp fluctuations in the market value of the Belarusian ruble and thus necessary and costly currency exchanges. Consequently payments to the Russian Federation must usually be in hard currency or in Russian rubles.[7]

Cut-rate Russian petroleum is important, as Belarus had always refined the imported oil it did not need domestically for profitable sale in the West. By the calculation of one Belarusian economist, that subsidy amounted to $72 billion from 2000–2015, about one year's GDP![8] Of course, any cheaper oil and gas would change the game for Minsk. As of 2018 Belarus owes a large (though disputed) bill to Russia for oil and gas, because Moscow has refused to cut the price charged to Belarus to that for European buyers. To Moscow's refusal Minsk responded by raising the pipeline transport charge for Russian petroleum by 8 percent. In reply Russia has even cut off supply temporarily from the Gazprom-owned pipeline that traverses Belarus. Now a higher extraction tax unfavorable to Belarus is being negotiated. Nevertheless, Belarus is paying on previous loans from Russia.

Relations with the Russian Federation

The unpredictable actions of authoritarian President Aleksandr Lukashenko, who has ruled Belarus since 1994, has also made the country unattractive to Putin for business or investments except as a place to station troops.[9] Lukashenko denies that Moscow has any "base" in his country, although Belarus participates in the Russian Federation air defense system, and Russia conducts military training and exercises on Belarusian territory. The large CSTO Zapad exercises of 2017 were based there.

Belarus has stood up to its powerful eastern neighbor on many occasions. Like several other CIS countries, Lukashenko's government opposed Russian annexation of Crimea and its military intervention in Ukraine. At the 2017 meeting in Minsk of the OSCE Belarus joined ninety other members in condemning Putin's actions in Ukraine; only Armenia dissented. Lukashenko refused to sign a new EaEU customs code in late 2016 drawn up at a summit meeting from which the Belarusian President absented himself. By other abrasive demonstrations, he loudly proclaims Belarusian independence. The Belarusian ruler seems quite interested in closer ties with the EU, which already sends him cash through the European Neighborhood Policy. Because of its open eastern border Belarus suffered along with Russia from the EU sanctions.[10] Since Russia imposed counter-sanctions on EU agricultural products, Belarus has served as a conduit through which those products have been able to enter Russia. As a result, unusually large shipments of apples and fruit from Ukraine and Poland seem to have found their way to Russian consumers. Fine French cheese has also been smuggled into Russia, obviously through Belarus.[11] Occasional disputes over customary Belarusian dairy, beef, and pork exports to Russia have angered Belorusians. More recently Lukashenko accused Russia of unfairly subsidizing its downtrodden agriculture, using these words, "The Russians are behaving barbarically (*varvarski*) towards us, and I'm speaking publicly about this."[12] In a more tangible answer a large Chinese industrial park was opened not long ago in Minsk.

The usual pattern of behavior between these two close neighbors is for Putin to refuse various initiatives from Lukashenko, or the reverse, leaving these two countries in uneasy coexistence. For example, the Lukashenko government introduced visa-free entry to Western citizens for five days in 2017, permitting their easy rail trip to Russia; Moscow responded, instituting unilateral border controls. Reading the controlled press from Minsk makes the Lukashenko regime's resentment of Russian treatment very clear. In the Russian press rumors of plots to remove the Belarusian leader appear commonly. But major urban demonstrations against a new tax in March, 2017, apparently did not involve Russia. In April 2017, Putin "congratulated his Belarusian counterpart Lukashenko, on the Day of Unity of the Russian and Belarusian People and . . . gave high praise to integration results. . . . There are no unresolved issues."[13]

The most important aspects of the Russian-Belarussian relationship in Putin's eyes are maintaining Belarussian membership in the EaEU and ensuring Belarussian security cooperation vis-à-vis NATO. Despite the continually arising disagreements between the two countries, Putin has succeeded in achieving these objectives. One might say in view of their frequent disputes that Putin cannot live with Lukashenko—or live without him.

THE BALTIC STATES

Estonia, Latvia, and Lithuania have shared similar experiences for a long time. Independent states from 1920–1939, they were occupied by Nazi Germany during World War II. After liberation by the Red Army, all three were unwillingly attached to the Soviet Union as "union republics." Dissatisfied with this status and preferring a Western orientation, Balts staged several mass demonstrations during the 1980s.[14] Finally in 1990–1991 they were the first republics to exit the USSR. Russia withdrew most of its troops from the Baltics in 1993–1994, and the Baltic countries eagerly signed up for NATO's Partnership for Peace. But only in 1998 did Russia officially terminate its military presence in the Baltics, when it decommissioned its Skrunda-1 radar station in Latvia. The last Russian soldier left the region in October 1999.[15]

By now each Baltic country has settled its borders with the others and with Russia, including an arrangement for passage through Lithuania to Russia's Kaliningrad outpost. These settlements allowed them to enter the EU and NATO in 2004. Some mutual suspicions, disagreements on water borders and fishing rights, and competition for outside investments, however, prevent closer ties among the three small countries.

Demography

These three countries have populations of only 1.3 to 2.8 million, including sizable Russian minorities. In Latvia 26 percent of residents are ethnic Russians, in Estonia 25 percent, and in Lithuania 6 percent now. At independence the Russian percentage was close to half in Latvia, thirty percent in Estonia, and twenty percent in Lithuania. This decline reflects departures of some loyal Communists who had been sent there in Soviet times, as well as many other Russians who felt discouraged about their prospects with Balts in power. Tens of thousands of Baltic Russians, who were granted EU citizenship after 2004, chose to move to the UK and Ireland, where they were welcomed owing to labor shortages. In part to combat this movement, in 2012 Russia initiated a repatriation program to resettle ethnic Russians living abroad. These days the Russian-speakers remaining in the Baltics are concentrated in the three capitals (Tallinn, Riga, and Vilnius) and in small enclaves closer to the Russian Federation border, such as Idi-Varu (Narva) in Estonia; Latgale (Dauvpils) in Latvia; and Zarasai (Visaginas) in Lithuania.

A major impetus for Russians to leave has been the efforts of Baltic governments to induce their ethnic Russian residents to use the (quite different) Baltic languages, rather than Russian. This problem has been most acute in Latvia, where ethnic Latvians constituted only a bare majority of the population at the time of independence. Many Latvians feared cultural assimilation by Russians, even linguistic extinction. Accordingly, there was (and remains) widespread opposition to widespread use of Russian in public life. In 2012, voters thus opposed making Russian a second official language. Despite contrary advice from Western partners, Latvia requires the Latvian language to be used for all official functions (but not for all public events). The Russian annexation of Crimea and intervention in Eastern Ukraine in 2014 aggravated the situation: Putin justified these steps as undertaken to defend the rights of Russian speakers there. Latvians fear a repetition of these events in their own country. A new law, passed in 2018, aims to limit the use of Russian in schools, mandating that all instruction in the last three years of high school be conducted in Latvian. The Russian Foreign Ministry has reacted angrily, calling this legislation "odious."[16] Putin has threatened sanctions, thus far to no avail. In fact, a new law against teaching in non-EU languages in Latvian universities is also under consideration.[17] On account of Latvia's notably strict language requirements for naturalization, many older Russians living there remain stateless.

The situation is better for ethnic Russians in Estonia and Lithuania, where the demographic advantage of the titular nationality was much greater at the time of independence, and fear of cultural and linguistic extinction was therefore not as intense. While the Estonian government, like the Lithuanian, has made a language test required for citizenship for Russians who arrived after 1940, over time Tallinn made those tests less challenging. The government has also reached out to its Russian population in other ways. The Estonian President made a much publicized visit to the Russian enclave of Narva, located on the border of Russia, and there has been some effort to channel investment into this city.[18] With EU help the government has constructed a river walkway along the border there. (Cynics say that the purpose is to enable people to see what less prosperous Russia looks like.) Lithuania, where ethnic Russians have always been a smaller, and thus less threatening minority, has done less to offend and antagonize Moscow in this matter. In contrast to the other two Baltic governments, Vilnius has granted citizenship to all citizens who desire it, not imposing any language requirements.

Economy

Except during the 2008–2009 world financial crisis, all three Baltic nations have prospered under independence. They have registered per capita GDP levels of $28–32,000 and growth rates of 2 to 5 percent since 2014.[19] Aside from energy from some hydropower, oil shale, and peat, they must import liquid fuels and natural gas from Russia.[20] As of 2014–2015 they all use the euro currency and enjoy low inflation rates, but also fairly high unemployment and out-migration. All three countries have small manufactures and agricultural specialties. All three trade with Russia, as well as with close neighbors. Tourism with Westerners is active via the Baltic Sea ports.

Relations with the Russian Federation

After several years of associate status in the European Union, Estonia, Latvia, and Lithuania joined the organization in 2004. Russia initially welcomed that expansion.[21] On the other hand, NATO membership was strongly protested by Russia even before it occurred. As early as 1997, when the alliance began discussion of which East European states would be the first to be invited, Moscow made it clear that admission of the Baltics was completely unacceptable. Foreign Minister Yevgeny Primakov declared publicly that "Russia cannot be indifferent to…the Baltic countries' proximity to our vital centers . . . not only our strategic missiles, but also tactical aircraft."[22] One might ask, as Putin undoubtedly did in 2004, against whom is this expansion directed? As mentioned earlier, this move was directly contrary to promises made to the United States government. In response, Russian leaders began emphasizing that the entire "former Soviet space" was in their sphere of influence.[23] Putin warned that Russia would be closely monitoring any deployment of NATO forces in the Baltics and would adjust its defense and security policies as needed to deal with such threatening steps.[24]

Putin has pledged to support the Russian-speaking minorities in the Baltic countries, where many ex-Soviet officials, industrial workers and their families had been living for years before those countries became independent. Many older Russians belong to NGOs organized by Russki Mir (Russian World), a government-sponsored organization Putin created by decree in 2007 in order to promote the Russian language outside Russia. Regular Russian-language broadcasts to the Baltic area feature entertainment popular with their audiences, as well as news commentaries favorable to Moscow's point of view, which often exaggerates discrimination against Russian ethnics. These broadcasts were stepped up in the aftermath of Russia's intervention in Ukraine so that ethnic Russians could be exposed to Moscow's perspective on the conflict. They heard a very different version of the events than ethnic Balts were hearing from their governments.

Moscow's efforts to build support for its actions in Ukraine appear to have enjoyed a measure of success among Russians in the Baltics. Some have expressed sympathy with Putin's protection of the Crimean and East Ukrainian Russians. But most Balts see little reason for such protection in their countries.[25] "After decades of hearing lies from Moscow, 'we're vaccinated,' says Eeva Eek-Pajuste of the International Centre for Defense and Security, a think-tank in Tallinn. Most disbelieve anything that sounds Putin-ny."[26]

With Moscow's encouragement, Russians in the Baltics have been politically active. This is especially the case in Latvia and Estonia, where government policies have been more restrictive of their rights. These voters support parties that back expanding the role of Russian, citizenship for all long-term residents, and stronger ties with Russia. Latvia's Harmony Centre political party, backed by most Russians, won 20 percent of the vote in the 2018 election, but will not be permitted by the other parties to join the government, even though it no longer cooperates with Putin's United Russia Party and has joined with the European-leaning parties' stand approving sanctions against Russia.[27] By contrast, the Estonian Centre Party, supported by nearly all Russians in the country, has participated in the government on two occasions in the past, and its head, Juri Ratas, is currently Prime Minister.

Occasionally, Russia has had open disagreements with the Baltic States. In 2007 Estonia proposed removing a Soviet war memorial from its prominent place in the capital, Tallinn. In response, a cyber-attack from Russia temporarily disabled Estonia's electronic banking and many government functions.[28] When Lithuania outlawed Communist symbols, that country also suffered a cyber-attack. Numerous hybrid and "fake news" broadcasts believed to originate from Russia have been reported by all of the Baltic countries, especially since the Russian intervention in Crimea and the Donbas in 2014. Employing the kind of "hybrid warfare" he has relied on in Ukraine, Putin has used the internet in the Baltics to sow discontent with the governments there. Russian-financed Sputnik News has expanded coverage in the region since 2016, broadcasting in all three Baltic languages so as to reach non-Russians as well as Russians.[29]

Russia has employed not only cyber-weapons, but also what is sometimes called its "energy weapon" in the Baltics. When officials in Vilnius pressed for investigation of Gazprom's monopoly practices within the EU, Gazprom retaliated by raising its price for gas delivered to Lithuania through the distribution network of this government-owned company (Lithuania still pays more for energy than does Germany). Far more dependent on Russian gas, Latvia has also been a target of Moscow's energy weapon. Learning from such disputes, each Baltic state has developed a facility to guarantee gas if Russia were to cut it off suddenly. Lithuania opened an LNG facility at Klaipeda, for example.

Since the events in Crimea and Ukraine, these countries bordering the Russian Federation have felt a threat to their independence and have urged NATO to increase their defense capabilities. The alliance has responded with an air shield operated from air bases in Poland (Malbork), Estonia, and Lithuania. Brussels has also adopted a new "Enhanced Forward Presence Policy." In July 2017 Estonia and Latvia agreed to the stationing of NATO troops on their territories. They train in guerrilla tactics. The presidents of all three Baltic States visited U.S. President Donald Trump early in 2018 to voice their worries over Putin's actions and to reinforce their claims to protection under the NATO joint defense concept. As of 2018, four new multinational battalions from 19 NATO countries are stationed in the Baltic countries and Poland.[30] Analysts have described the new strategy as the "porcupine approach": these forces are not able to defeat the vast numbers of Russian troops that could be deployed against them, but they are sufficient to make the host countries "highly unattractive to occupy."[31]

Moscow's response has been to build up its forces in its Western Military District, bordering on the Baltics and Finland. A key element in this buildup has been Kaliningrad, a small but strategically vital enclave on the Baltic Sea coast wedged between Lithuania and Poland. The build-up became noticeable beginning in 2016, when Russia began moving mobile short-range offensive ballistic missiles into this territory. These missiles can reach all of the Baltics, as well as two-thirds of Poland. They are particularly intimidating because they can carry nuclear, as well as conventional, warheads.[32] Moscow has also been building up the size of its air forces in Kaliningrad and adding additional submarines to its nearby Baltic fleet. NATO sees these deployments as part of a Russian strategy of "anti-access/area denial." In the event of a Russian move against any of the Baltic States, these weapons could prevent NATO reinforcements from moving to the front to defend those states. More recently, in the first part of 2018, Russia also sent thousands of new troops to its borders with Latvia, Estonia and Finland, as well as Kaliningrad. These were accompanied by five thousand new and modernized weapons and equipment.[33]

Escalation continues. A large naval exercise around Norway—called "Trident Juncture"—occurred in late 2018 with all 29 NATO members participating, plus Finland and Sweden. The entire "Bucharest Nine" on NATO's eastern flank have asked for reinforcements.[34] In turn, the expansion of NATO's collective security arrangements appears to have motivated Russia to increase the scale of its Zapad (western) military exercises near the borders with the Baltic States, as well as with Finland.

As is the case with regard to Belarus, Putin's policy toward the Baltic States can at best be described as partially successful. The Baltics are the place where the disintegration of the USSR began. From that time on, there was always a perceived threat that the Baltic model—a complete and decisive turn to the West and refusal to participate in any organization led by

Russia—would be followed by other states in the Near Abroad. For Putin, such a development would undermine his aspiration to restore Russia's great power status through Moscow's domination of the Near Abroad. In fact, the rebellion of the Baltics has not given rise to this nightmare scenario. No other states in the Near Abroad have followed the path taken by the Balts. That is as much a result of Western reluctance to embrace those other states as it is a product of astute Russian policy.

As we have seen in the discussion above, for Putin there are three principal issues in Russia's relations with the Baltics: their treatment of Russians residing there; the role of the EU in promoting and reinforcing democratic values in this region; and the growing presence and activity of NATO. The treatment of Russians is important for Putin because Russian nationalists at home, who are politically influential, are important constituents of his, and they care deeply about the fate of their compatriots abroad. Putin has had to ensure that the Russians who choose to remain in the Baltics are able to find employment and, at least gradually, receive social acceptance and obtain political influence. That has been happening, ironically, as much as a result of EU pressure on the governments of the Baltic States, as of any actions taken by Moscow.

The democratic values and the democratic model that the EU promotes in the Baltics have had some attraction for people in nearby Belarus, Ukraine, and Moldova, but the authoritarian regime in Belarus has prevented democratic development there, and the experiment with democracy in Ukraine and Moldova has been so burdened by corruption as to limit its attractiveness in Russia (Putin's ultimate concern). NATO's presence in the Baltic States has been sufficiently limited, even in the aftermath of the events in Ukraine in 2014, as to constitute more a symbolic and a psychological threat than a real military problem for Russia. In sum, despite their potential for doing so, the Baltics have not, in fact, posed a serious challenge to Putin's aims in the Near Abroad since their "defection" in 2004.

FINLAND

A Nordic state, Finland has close connections with the Baltic countries, especially Estonia, with which it shares a Finno-Ugric language. Easy transportation across the narrow Gulf of Finland joins its capital Helsinki with Tallinn, the attractive Estonian capital.

Finland has had a long history of dealing with its Russian neighbor. From 1809 to 1917 it was a Grand Duchy of the Russian Empire, but it became an independent republic after World War I. Stalin's army invaded Finland in 1939; after a bitter war, it was forced to cede territory northwest of Leningrad (now St. Petersburg) to the Soviet Union and to sign a mutual defense treaty in 1948. When the USSR collapsed in 1991, Helsinki abrogated that and other treaties and reassumed its prior obligations. But like its neighbor Sweden, Finland did not attempt to join NATO.[35] Given the geographical proximity to St. Petersburg, that would have been seen as highly provocative. More recently, however, Finland has quietly converted its army to NATO equipment and contributed troops to NATO missions. In 2006 it joined the EU battle group and in 2008 added to a NATO response group. Cooperation has intensified in the aftermath of the crisis in Ukraine. In May, 2018, Finland signed an agreement with the United States allowing Finnish troops to participate in NATO drills in exchange for granting NATO access to its territory and military infrastructure.[36] Officially, however, the Republic of Finland remains neutral.

Economy

Finland is a wealthy country (GDP per capita of over $40,000) with successful electronics and scientific instrument companies, machinery, and wood pulp and paper industries. In 1995 Finland joined the European Union and now uses the euro currency. Finland imports raw materials from Russia.

Relations with the Russian Federation

Owing to the proximity of its population centers, Finland depends heavily on Russia for natural gas and some electricity. Relations with Russia are normal, though sometimes the border crossing near Vyborg can be troublesome. Like the other Baltic nations, Finland has to tolerate Russian airspace and cyber intrusions. An unknown number of Russian secret police are said to reside in the country. Air defense systems have been stationed by Russia on the Kola Peninsula, east of Finland and Sweden.

The 833-mile border between Finland and Russia briefly became the site of a major refugee crisis for Helsinki in 2015–2016. Thousands of refugees from Afghanistan and the Middle East obtained Russian visas, flew to Russia, and from there made their way into Finland, with some crossing into Norway. For a while, Russia looked the other way, and then blocked their return. The Finns were furious and demanded to meet with Russian officials at the highest level. The crisis was resolved only when Putin himself intervened in support of a border security agreement, negotiated with Finland's center-right government of Prime Minister Juha Sipilä. The episode was emblematic of the determination of both sides to avoid any serious deterioration of their relationship. Putin has a major stake in the preservation of Finland's neutral status, which has prevented the entry of NATO troops into the territory of yet another country on Russia's border.[37] Finland does not want to provoke the Russian Bear.

CONCLUSION

Putin's inability to prevent the accession of the Baltic States to NATO despite his government's frequent warnings that such a step would violate his country's vital interests represents his greatest policy failure in the Near Abroad. However, his success in retaining the security cooperation of strategically-located Belarus and his deployment of Russian military assets in Ukraine have helped to prevent further eastward expansion of the Atlantic alliance. In other words, Putin's policies since 2004 have kept NATO at bay, ensuring that it does not encroach further on what he regards as Russia's privileged sphere of influence. The Russian President has also succeeded in maintaining Finnish neutrality, thereby helping to secure Russia's northwestern border.

NOTES

1. In 1998 presidents Boris Yeltsin and Aleksandr Lukashenko signed a declaration of their intent to form a "union state" within a year.

2. Donaldson, Robert H., Joseph L. Nogee, and Vidya Nadkarni, *The Foreign Policy of Russia*, 5th ed. (Sharpe, 2014), 84.

3. *World Bank* estimate of July 26, 2018.

4. The Chernobyl nuclear reactor is located on Ukraine's border with Belarus. Seventy percent of the fallout from the accident landed in Belarus, heavily contaminating one-fourth of the country and seriously affecting 7 million people. Twenty percent of Belarus' annual budget is devoted to dealing with the resulting costs. Kim Hjelmgaard, "In secretive Belarus, Chernobyl's impact is breathtakingly grim," *USA Today*, April 17, 2016.

5. *World Almanac 2018*, 753. The World Almanac 2019 gives an unbelievable rate of 0.5 percent. [sic, 753]

6. *The Economist*, January 12, 2019.

7. *Izvestia*, December 4, 2017; *Nezavisimaia Gazeta*, December 27, 2017.

8. Quoting an estimate by Aleksandr Chubrik. Yevgeny Karasyuk in *Republic.ru,* February 20, 2017. CD 69, no. 8–9: 17.

9. This was permitted under a treaty on cooperation and friendship of 1994, ratified by Minsk in 1995. Without assistance from these forces Lukashenko crushed a massive protest following his third re-election in 2010. Another protest against a tax on the unemployed and general economic conditions was suppressed in 2017.

10. The EU lifted these sanctions on Belarus in 2015.

11. Bruno Macçãs, *The Dawn of Eurasia* (New Haven, CT: Yale University Press, 2018), 189.

12. "Notebook: A Roundup of Some of the Latest News from Russia," *Russian Life (*November-December, 2018): 9.

13. Nina Ilyina, *Vedomosti,* April 5, 2017. CD 69, no.14: 16. Prime Minister Medvedev has said that a Union State central bank and courts are "being considered."

14. Romuald J. Misiunas and Rein Taagepera, *The Baltic States: Years of Dependence, 1940–1990* (Berkeley and Los Angeles: University of California Press,1993), 290–315. Notable among these were the Tallinn demonstration in April 1988 against the Molotov-Ribbentrop Pact and the "Singing Revolution" of a half million Balts in a human chain marking fifty years of "illegal" Soviet rule. In 1990 after Lithuania signed the "Act on the Re-Establishment of the State of Lithuania," provoking a lethal attack by Soviet tanks on "Bloody Sunday," fifty thousand Lithuanians barricaded the Supreme Council building. Subsequently an overwhelming referendum approved reestablishing that country's independence.

15. "Russia Pulls Last Troops Out of the Baltics," *Moscow Times*, October 22, 1999.

16. Lucian Kim, "A New Law in Latvia Aims to Preserve National Language by Limiting Russian in Schools," *NPR*, October 28, 2018.

17. Alec Kuhn, "Moscow threatens sanctions against Latvia over removal of Russian from secondary schools," *The Telegraph*, April 3, 2018.

18. "Estonia reaches out to its very own Russians at long last," *Deutsche Welle*, February 24, 2018.

19. *World Development Indicators 2016,* Table 4. *World Almanac 2019*, 774, 797, and 800.

20. Formerly Russia exported much of its gas through Latvia, but after 2000 it built new terminals near St. Petersburg to do this—a penalty for Latvia's joining NATO. The Nordstream lines to Germany also circumvent these three states, as well as Ukraine.

21. 21 Sergei Yastrzhembsky, an aide to President Putin, stated that "Russia regards the expansion of the European Union as a good thing, positive for Russia, leading to the expansion of the zone of stability . . . the development of democracy, and the adoption of European legal standard in states immediately bordering Russia." *The New York Times*, September 5, 2004.

22. CD 49, no.9:19. Cited in Donaldson and Nadkarni, 5th ed., 233.

23. Vladimir Socor, " Kremlin Refining Policy in 'Post-Soviet Space,'" *Eurasia Daily Monitor*, February 8, 2005.

24. Steven Lee Meyers, "As NATO Finally Arrives on Its Borders, Russia Grumbles," *New York Times*, April 3, 2004.

25. Agnia Grigas, *Beyond Crimea: The New Russian Empire* (New Haven, CT: Yale University Press, 2016), chapter 5.

26. *The Economist*, February 2, 2019.

27. *The Economist,* October 13, 2018.

28. Estonia has resorted to an innovative approach to protecting itself from more such attacks. It has established what it calls a "data embassy" in Luxembourg, where online data crucial to the functioning of the government and the country's infrastructure will be stored. "Estonia buoys cyber security with world's first data embassy," *Deutsche Welle*, June 8, 2017.

29. "Baltics battle Russia in online disinformation war," *Deutsche Welle*, October 8, 2017.

30. They are "small enough not to provoke Russia but big enough to deter it. 'It's brilliant,' says a Latvian spook." The U.S. contingent helps with intelligence. *The Economist,* February 2, 2019.

31. "NATO in Baltics learns from Ukraine's mistakes," *Deutsche Welle,* August 2, 2017, citing analyst Michael Kofman of the Center for Naval Analyses.

32. With a range of more than three hundred miles, these missiles arguably fell within the purview of the Intermediate Range Nuclear Forces Treaty. Now that the United States has suspended its membership in this treaty, these missiles are more likely to remain in Kaliningrad on a permanent basis.

33. Tom O'Connor, "Russia Has Sent Thousands of Troops and Weapons to Its Western Border, Near U.S. Military and NATO Allies," *Newsweek*, July 24, 2018.

34. *Radio Free Europe/Radio Liberty*, June 12, 2018.

35. Under Prime Minister Sefan Löfven, Sweden "has maneuvered as close to the alliance as it is possible to get from the outside." *The Economist*, October 6, 2018. It has signed defense cooperation agreements with both NATO (in 2016) and the United States in 2017. Sweden also shares surveillance data and defense attachés with Norway, a NATO member. Some 2200 Swedish troops joined NATO exercises late in 2018. Sweden has reintroduced its military draft for men and women. Thomas Nilsen, "Northern Sweden and Finland play key role as NATO kicks off Trident Juncture," *The Barents Observer,* October 23, 2018.

36. O'Connor, *Newsweek.* Sweden signed a similar agreement at that time.

37. Reid Standish, "For Finland and Norway, the Refugee Crisis Heats Up Along the Russian Arctic," *Foreign Policy*, January 26, 2016; "Flow of migrants into Finland from Russia dries up," Reuters, March 17, 2016.

Chapter Seven

Russia v. China: A Problematic Partnership

The People's Republic of China (PRC) is undoubtedly the most important neighbor of the Russian Federation today. This large and powerful nation shares a border of 2,615 miles with Russia, more than any other neighboring country except Kazakhstan. With a population of 1.38 billion (nine times more than that of Russia), China is also the most populous. Despite some efforts to reduce births, China's population has grown some 19 percent from 1992 to 2019.

CHINA'S ECONOMIC GROWTH

Having grown in output rapidly since the 1979, China now produces some 15 percent of world GDP, second only to the United States.[1] China's aggregate output of $13.4 trillion is more than eight times larger than Russia's $1.6 trillion as of 2018, though China's per capita GDP of $9,608 is still about 15 percent lower.[2] The defense budget of the PRC is more than $150 billion, about one-third of the United States total but far larger than Russia's.[3] Among other things, this supports armed forces numbering 2.2 million, two and a half times that of the Russian total.

In the last thirty years China's rapid growth in the production of steel and other metals has depended a great deal on its coal deposits, but since the 2000s China has relied on oil imports for its rapidly growing automobile and bus fleets. Oil and gas, plus a new interest in solar power, promise to limit the heavy air (and water) pollution affecting several of China cities, including the capital in Beijing (population 22 million). Most of this oil and gas is obtained from Iran and Saudi Arabia by sea and from Central Asia via pipelines that extend as far west as Turkmenistan. Gazprom is now resuming construction of the *Sila Sibiri* ("Power of Siberia") natural gas pipeline from Russia to China with an underwater passage across the Amur River.[4] This formidable project is scheduled to open in late-2019. These land routes are considered safer than those from the Persian Gulf, which pass through the narrow Straits of Malacca and are liable to be controlled by Western navies in time of conflict.

The quadrupling of Chinese production has benefitted millions of Chinese poor who have moved to expanding cities, many on the coast. It also allowed an expansion and modernization of Chinese factories and infrastructure—railroads and airports, especially. Robotics, solar panels, automobiles, and electronic gear all have become world-class exportables for the PRC. Consequently, China is now in a position to conduct cyberwarfare, engage in naval maneuvers in the South China Sea, and invest billions in Russia's Near Abroad as well as elsewhere throughout Eurasia and beyond under the auspices of its vast Belt and Road Initiative (BRI). These assertions of China's power have added to Russians' long-standing fear of a "yellow peril" from a country they have begun to appreciate only recently. In light of its troubled history in recent decades, the relationship between Russia and China requires careful scrutiny.

CHINA'S RELATIONSHIP WITH RUSSIA: A HISTORICAL PERSPECTIVE

The People's Republic of China (PRC) was the product of a long and bloody civil war between Communist and Nationalist forces that took place in two phases, from 1927–1937 and from 1945-1949. Between those two phases, the contending parties joined forces in an effort to expel Japanese invaders. In the course of the internal struggle, the Soviet Union aided the Chinese Communists in many ways,[5] but its assistance in the earlier period was not always welcome.[6] In the second phase, the Soviets actually gave significant support to both sides, hardly endearing themselves to their Chinese comrades.

Once the Communist forces under Mao Zedong vanquished the Nationalists and established the PRC, the USSR was the first country to recognize the "new China" and the government made its orientation to Moscow clear.

However, Mao always resented Soviet efforts to direct the policies of the Chinese Communists before they took power, especially the Soviets' insistence that their Chinese comrades cooperate with the Nationalists, and he never forgot Stalin's willingness to make deals with Nationalist leader Chiang Kai-shek and even assist him in various ways. Late in December 1949, Mao visited Moscow, declaring that the PRC was an "ally of the Soviet Union" as he sought Soviet political and economic support. Yet Stalin's reception of Mao was less than cordial: he required the victorious Chinese leader to wait weeks to see him and then accorded him only an extremely brief meeting. Russia refused to return any of the territory its Tsarist regime had gained in three treaties in the mid-nineteenth century from the weak Qing dynasty, as Lenin had promised to do.[7] The new PRC was also not allowed to regain Mongolia, once a province of imperial China,[8] probably because Stalin wanted a buffer state between the USSR and China.[9] He did agree to forego usage rights to China's Far Eastern Railroad and South Manchuria Railroad. He also reluctantly promised to evacuate a Soviet naval base at Port Arthur and relinquish Soviet control of the Chinese port of Dairen. In the end, however, Stalin could not bring himself to give up these strategically and economically vital assets, and the Soviets remained there, despite Chinese protests, until after his death. During its first years, Mao's regime was clearly the weaker party, badly in need of Soviet assistance. In the 1950's the USSR did invest very substantially in joint projects with China in Xinjiang (East Turkestan) and in the Chinese Eastern Railway, a flow of investment capital that would be reversed in recent years.

Events soon tested the Chinese Communists. In June 1950 the forces of Kim Il Sung's Democratic People's Republic of Korea (DPRK) crossed the 38th parallel in an attempt to unify the Korean peninsula under North Korean control. These troops were soon countered by a United Nations intervention, led by the United States. After an amphibious landing at Inchon, General Douglas MacArthur—despite warnings from both the Chinese and U.S. President Harry Truman—drove his troops close to the Yalu River boundary between North Korea and China. The Chinese army then entered the Korean War, apparently with the approval of Stalin.[10] A bloody stand-off finally led to the armistice of 1953, signed by the DPRK, the UN, and China. That left North Korea dependent on an extremely weary China and a Russia that had lost little in the conflict. The Soviets insisted that China pay "to the last ruble" for the weapons they had supplied to China during the war.[11]

Russia's aid to North Korea continued for decades. The Chinese too, concerned about the stability of the Communist regime there, also provided assistance. The Republic of Korea (South Korea), which did not sign the armistice, was dependent on American help. Thus the DPRK constituted a kind of buffer state for both Russia and China against American power. Worries about the situation on all sides deepened when Kim's regime instituted a nuclear weapons program. Both Russia and China favored denuclearization, but Russia was somewhat more willing to apply pressure on North Korea to halt its work on the program. With only a river border of some eleven miles with that country, Russia was less concerned than China about the possibility that such pressure would result in a massive outflow of refugees.

During the Khrushchev era (1954–1964), Russia and China became competitors for the allegiance of Third World states. Khrushchev's approach was to tout the advantages of Soviet central planning and offer economic aid to movements, leaders, and regimes that were ready to pledge loyalty to the USSR. China, on the other hand, sought to promote the People's Republic as the natural ally of all countries struggling to free themselves from imperialist domination. At the Bandung Conference in 1955, Chinese Premier Zhou Enlai proclaimed Chinese leadership of the "Third World," along with such non-aligned states as Yugoslavia. He condemned all forms of imperialism, including Soviet colonialism in Central Asia. Chinese and Soviet delegations to Third World countries would often follow one another in rapid succession, both bidding for the support of their hosts in this emerging rivalry. Many Communist parties around the world began to split over which patron to follow.

During the 1950s and 1960s, China tried to reclaim neighboring territories once possessed by its imperial dynasties. Chinese troops moved into Tibet in 1950 to establish control there. The USSR gave China substantial assistance, helping it transport personnel and equipment. However, when a rebellion erupted in 1959, the Soviets were far less supportive. Soviet media published many reports by Western news outlets criticizing China's actions. In 1958 China came close to war with the United States over Taiwan, the refuge of the Nationalists since 1949. Mao ordered the shelling of the Nationalist-controlled island of Jinmen without informing the Soviets. The Russians were furious, accusing the Chinese of war-mongering. The Chinese in return dubbed the Soviets timid "accommodationists" owing to their eagerness to avoid a clash with the United States. So fearful were the Soviets of Chinese militancy that they suspended delivery of promised nuclear weapons technology to the People's Republic in 1959. In the same year the USSR pointedly refrained from supporting China in its armed clashes with India over border territory claimed by both. Beijing condemned Moscow's "strange stand of neutrality." Most experts agree that this year was a turning point in the Sino-Russian relationship, the beginning of its transformation from tensely competitive to overtly hostile. [12]

Tensions with the Soviet Union increased steadily, fueled by ideological differences, personal rivalry between Mao and Khrushchev, and Chinese opposition to the Soviet leader's attempts to liberalize Communist rule in his own country. Mao claimed that he and the Chinese Communist Party were more qualified than Khrushchev and the Soviet party to lead the international Communist movement. The USSR reduced its aid to China, and in 1960 Khrushchev removed all that remained of the thousands of Russian economic advisers, scientists, and technicians the Soviets had sent to China. Relations continued to worsen, with unresolved border disputes aggravating the tensions. In 1969 Russian and Chinese troops clashed on the Amur River separating the two countries. During the ensuing decade, some fifty-two Soviet divisions were positioned on the Chinese border.

In part to counter Russian influence in Asia, U.S. President Richard Nixon visited Beijing in 1972 and then recognized the PRC as the sole legal representative of China—without, however, abandoning America's ties with and military support for Taiwan. Following a two-year leadership struggle after Mao's death in 1976, Deng Xiaoping became China's "paramount" leader. Deng's gradual, pragmatic policies modified many of Mao's cultural, political, and economic campaigns and opened China to trade and investment with the West. Centralized planning was deemphasized and market incentives instituted. Despite this liberalization, relations with Russia did not begin to improve until 1982, when the two countries agreed to begin a dialogue on normalizing their interactions.

When Mikhail Gorbachev became the Soviet leader in 1985, he made substantial efforts to resolve Russia's outstanding issues with China. He travelled to Russia's Far Eastern city of Vladivostok, near the border with China, replicating in reverse Mao's journey to Moscow in 1949. This highly symbolic show of deference to China's leadership was an attempt to compensate for the humiliating treatment accorded to Mao by Stalin. Gorbachev used the occasion to announce a remarkable series of concessions to the Chinese: withdrawal of Soviet troops from Mongolia, Russia's Far East, and

Afghanistan and acceptance of China's position regarding the location of the border between the USSR and China along the Amur and Ussuri Rivers.

This trip was followed by one to Beijing in 1989 for the first Sino-Russian summit in three decades. Gorbachev's arrival inspired a pro-democracy demonstration by tens of thousands of students in Tiananmen Square, with the protestors demanding "*glasnost*" or political openness of the kind the Soviet leader had brought to his country. While the summit resulted in an important agreement on normalization of Chinese-Russian relations, it also led to a mutual acknowledgement that the two sides were not seeking to harmonize their policies. The Chinese were highly skeptical of *glasnost*, which they viewed as likely to lead to loss of political control by the center. The following year Chinese Premier Li Peng (who had studied in the Soviet Union) went to Moscow with a ten-year pact which offered increased economic and scientific cooperation. These events signaled a major change of course between the two countries.

After the breakup of the USSR in 1991, Boris Yeltsin's presidency continued Russia's rapprochement with China while also cultivating good relations with the West. Moscow and Beijing issued a number of declarations of "partnership" and "equality," emphasizing (at Beijing's insistence) that there would be no return to the period in which Moscow claimed the right to direct China's policies. For the first time, China began to import Russian oil in 1993, providing much needed boost to Russia's deeply depressed economy at the time. Yeltsin's Foreign (and later Prime) Minister Yevgeny Primakov spoke repeatedly about the need to strengthen cooperation with the Asia-Pacific region, envisioning the possibility that Russia, China and India might even coordinate their actions. [13]

Soon after taking office in 2000, Yeltsin's chosen successor as President, Vladimir Putin, visited Beijing and proclaimed a "strategic partnership" with China—signaling his desire for a special relationship but one short of an alliance. Russia and China agreed to create the new Shanghai Cooperation Organization in 2001 (its development was described in Chapter 3). By 2004, Russia and China were able to resolve the remaining border issues by dividing the islands in the Amur River between them. Gradually bilateral trade increased, too, as the PRC had more hard cash available and could acquire Russian oil and gas needed for its continued expansion. By 2016, Russia became China's biggest supplier of these vital resources. By the early 2000s, when Russia's military industry was still faltering for lack of demand, China became Russia's biggest customers for arms. The world financial crisis of

2008, concentrated largely in Europe and the United States, may have convinced Russia and China to see each other as more dependable than the West. In 2011, with a visit of Chinese President Hu Jintao to Russia, the two countries could proclaim a "comprehensive strategic partnership of coordination."

By 2010 China had achieved the status of Russia's number one trade partner. Since 2014, the decline of Russia's trade with the European Union owing to sanctions and counter-sanctions has resulted in a steady increase in its trade with China. By 2017, this exchange had grown to 10 percent of Russia's total trade; by 2018 the figure was 15 percent.[14] As a consumer of imported energy, China has benefitted from reduced prices of oil and gas since 2014, while Russia, a major producer, has lost some profits, but it still benefits significantly from China's purchases. China has also become a major exporter of manufactured products to Russia (as well as to all of Central Asia), importing in exchange timber, petroleum, and food. Russia's trade follows the opposite pattern: it exports energy, materials, and food grains, and imports some machinery and consumer durables from China. This reflects a complementary trade relationship, although the nature of these tradables represents "neo-colonial imperialism" to Marxist-educated Russian elites. Russia sells few manufactured articles other than advanced weapons to the PRC, while China exports manufactured consumer goods, as well as a growing amount of specialized machinery, to Russia. However, although China takes some 10 percent of Russia's exports, Russia receives only about 2 percent of China's export sales.[15]

Russia is contributing to China's growing military strength. Among Beijing's major purchases have been the S-300 long-range surface-to-air missile system, T-72 tanks, submarines, and rocket launchers. In 2014 Putin announced a deal to sell China the much more sophisticated S-400 air defense system, possibly reflecting the increased utility to Moscow of its relationship with Beijing in the aftermath of moves by Western countries to limit their economic relationship with Russia and isolate it on the world stage.[16] Having bought fighter planes, too, China has directed its engineers to replicate, improve, and cheapen the Russian models, to the point that Beijing could sell them elsewhere, somewhat to Russia's displeasure. China did, however, buy twenty-four of Russia's highly sophisticated Su-35 long-range fighter planes in 2015, becoming the first foreign country to receive it.[17]

CHINA'S RELATIONS WITH THE RUSSIAN FEDERATION: BASIC INTERESTS

Unlike the neighbors we have surveyed in Chapters 4 and 5, present-day China does not pose either a threat of chaotic instability or a closer alliance with the West. Hence its political challenge is mostly intangible at present, and there are positive elements of complementarity, too. After all, geopolitical agreement, though intangible, is always appreciated. For both China and the Russian Federation, the United Nations as an institution represents a key component of multi-polarity in the international system, as opposed to what they regard as Western "hegemonial" influence. Both, on the other hand, reject the jurisdiction of international tribunals over disputes between two sovereign states. The two governments rarely disagree in their votes on the UN Security Council. Both states disparage "democratism," which they see as hypocritical. Instead of individual human rights, the touchstone of liberalism, Russia and China both emphasize group interests, as represented by the state. Courts are under the control of the central regime in both countries.

Until recently, Chinese investments in Russia were fairly insignificant, and that is still true of the reverse flow. Chinese investors have distrusted Russian legal protections, and Russian businessmen are uncomfortable with the Chinese language and the country's commercial practices. However, this relationship is changing. Chinese nuclear and electricity installations in Russia have been important since the early 2000s. Starting in 2016, moreover, Chinese investors have been playing a vital role in the oil, gas, LNG, and chemical industries of the Russian Federation. Besides the pipelines, joint ventures between the two countries were rare in the past. But now a deal between OAK of Russia and COMAC to build a large civilian aircraft has been announced. The engine will be Russian and the assembly will be in Shanghai.[18]

Still, the Russian goods market is much less important for China than that of the West, and this contributes to China's abiding interest in good relations with the United States and Europe as well as with Russia. According to Shi Zi, a former Chinese diplomat, China benefits from the present international system. "We want to improve it and modify it, not to break it." By contrast, he said, Russia thinks it is victimized by that system.[19]

Both Russia and China fear any incursion of radical Islamists, terrorists, or rebels from Muslim minorities long resident within their borders.[20] They both stoutly defend their external borders and existing territorial sovereignty on land or sea. Sitting permanently on the UN Security Council, they each proclaim a commitment to their neighbors' borders and sovereignty.[21] Hence, the Chinese have refrained from endorsing Russian invasions and occupations in Georgia, the Crimea, and eastern Ukraine. Like Russia, China is also interested in keeping Western ideas away from its population. Any organized expression of minority nationalism ("separatism"), alien religions, or open claim for broader human rights is rejected and can lead to imprisonment in either country. The Xinjiang-Uighur Autonomous Region, a large, lightly populated area of northwestern China on the border with Kazakhstan, Kyrgyzstan, and Tajikistan, commands special attention from Beijing because of its Uighur Muslim minority. Occasional protests and armed outbreaks in Xinjiang have been met with force, increased Han immigration, infrastructure investments, and sinicization of the traditional Turkic culture. The 2009 clashes between Han and Uighur men on the streets of Urumqi may have triggered intensive Chinese policing to eradicate Muslim and Uighur language and culture there since Xi Jinping became President and head of the Communist Party. Mostly recently "re-education" camps have been set up for an estimated one million Muslim Uighurs. The situation in China is somewhat comparable to the Kremlin's sensitivity to Muslim unrest in the Caucasian region and its Russification efforts there.

CURRENT RELATIONS BETWEEN CHINA AND RUSSIA

While relations between the two countries have varied widely in the past and were even quite hostile at times, the current situation is relatively stable at present, with both countries pursuing their own national interests while avoiding affront to the other. The Russian "pivot" to Asia, notable since 2014, seems permanent, as long as the NATO countries refuse to recognize the Crimean annexation or accept Russia's military involvement in Ukraine. As of 2019, Vladimir Putin and Xi Jinping have a working friendship and have met many times. Commercial and diplomatic cooperation is maintained in world institutions, with common opposition to most initiatives put forward by the United States. For instance, Russia and China have taken similar or complementary positions on cyber-warfare, human rights, Iran, and North Korea. Both forbid the presence of foreign NGOs. It even seems that official Chinese news agencies have been ordered to improve coverage of Putin's Russia. Chinese Foreign Minister Wang Yi has said that the relationship with Russia is at the "best level in history." Russian Foreign Minister Sergei

Lavrov has said that the two countries have no conflicts with regard to Central Asia. Chinese investments in Central Asia do not yet disturb the Russians politically and they contribute to desirable economic stability there.

Security cooperation is growing. The two countries have been holding joint naval exercises in the Pacific and the Mediterranean. For the first time Russia has invited the PRC to participate in military exercises in the Far East. Its Vostok 18 exercise included 3,200 Chinese troops, among the roughly seventy-five thousand participants.[22] At that time Russian Defense Minister Sergei Shogiu called the Chinese "allies." We think this a friendly exaggeration.[23] With similar views expressed in many of Russia's and Chinese policy stances, though, it's not surprising that public opinion among Russian citizens about China has significantly improved, as shown in Levada Center surveys since 2016.[24] Russians undoubtedly benefit, perhaps unknowingly, from the shuttle trade that has brought vast amounts of shoes and clothing (often counterfeited brands) to open-air markets in Moscow and elsewhere. According to Sergei Karaganov, a former Kremlin advisor, "For the foreseeable future we are going to be very close partners, de facto allies with China, even though there will never be a formal alliance."[25]

Despite the mutual compliments, however, there are some potential differences and sources of tension between the two countries. China abstained from a UN General Assembly resolution (68/262) condemning Russia's annexation of Crimea. Russia doesn't endorse Chinese claims in the South China Sea, while China rejects Russian claims of sovereignty in the Arctic, where Moscow has already established some military outposts. Opening a usable northern route would cut transport time from China to Europe, and President Xi said that China wishes to become a "great polar power." In all likelihood, Moscow does not welcome such competition, even from a strategic partner. In his report to the 2017 Communist Party Congress, Xi asserted that "we should . . . oppose acts that impose one's will on others . . . as well as the practice of the strong bullying the weak." This could apply to Russia as well as the United States. As evidence of that posture, China has refused to support Russia in about half of the Security Council resolutions dealing with Syria.[26]

China has been a careful shopper for energy. As shown in tortuous negotiations with Moscow, China insisted on paying market rates for natural gas despite the unusually high costs in constructing a pipeline through Siberia. The recurrence of low energy prices, as we have discussed in Chapter 2, would aggravate the economic asymmetry between China as consumer and

Russia as provider. The May 2014, deal to sell natural gas to China took a decade to negotiate because of the cost of the length of the pipeline involved as well as the price to be charged. The deal was signed only in 2014, when natural gas prices were falling. Some observers expect that China will decrease its attention to sources of oil, relying instead on natural gas from Siberia, LNG from Australia and elsewhere, and even its own (as yet little developed) shale gas reserves. With much lower world oil and gas prices expected, China may well decide to rely on normal market sources instead of negotiated production deals funded by infrastructure investments. [27]

Another potential issue has to do with sparsely settled Siberian lands on the Russian side of the border set in 1689 (and demarcated more recently) along the Argun, Amur, and Issuri rivers. [28] China has heavily populated northern regions which are short of crop and grazing lands; Russians have been leaving this difficult and remote area for years, reportedly at a rate of about a million a year. Russia's tariffs and export taxes are just two of the impediments to citizens there. Since the Russian state owns and manages almost all of the potential resources in Siberia and the Far East, its "low competence" and corrupt officialdom make foreign investment there unattractive. [29] China is building bridges to Siberia and has suggested a "free trade area" in the region. Reportedly about a million and a half Chinese entered the Russian Far East in 2013, and official sources warn that Chinese could be a majority there within two or three decades. [30] Eyewitness estimates are that 400,000–550,000 Chinese live in Russia, though many are in the more dynamic Western part. [31] Many Russians are uneasy about these migrants to the Far East and what they might mean for Moscow's control of the region in the future.

What about an exchange of arable land? A Chinese company offered to buy more than 100,000 hectares of Siberian land but was refused. At a conference in St. Petersburg in 2014 Chinese Vice President Li Yuan-chao proposed joint development of land in Siberia and northeast China but met with silence from Russian representatives. [32] But by 2015, when things had changed dramatically, Russian diplomats have cautiously welcomed infrastructure investments there. Chinese banks are reluctant to invest in sizeable projects in this area, however, leaving only small manufacturing and some farms. [33] Were China to take on projects in Siberia, very likely the Chinese population presence would be temporary since most Chinese prefer the better wages and more familiar cultural and linguistic environment of the PRC.

CURRENT CHINESE FOREIGN POLICY

Until 2008 China assumed an openly modest place in world affairs. This was the era of China's "peaceful rise," as Chinese leaders described their policy. Deng Xiaoping (who retired from his position as "paramount leader" in 1992) urged China to "hide its strength and bide its time." Accordingly, China joined in multilateral declarations stressing non-intervention, opposition to separatism, and a multi-polar world order. Deng's immediate successor, Jiang Xemin, Party leader from 1989–2002, did little to change this posture. China joined the World Trade Organization in 2001 and helped to found the Shanghai Cooperation Organization in the same year. The SCO was intended to bolster global multi-polarity (see Chapter 3).

What changed this approach to the world appears to have been the worldwide financial crisis of 2008. The restraint that had characterized China's policy under Deng and Jiang had been predicated on the belief that China did not yet occupy a strong position in the global balance of power. After 2008, Chinese leaders perceived that balance to be shifting in China's favor, and Hu Jintao, General Secretary of the Party from 2002-2012, resolved to change China's policy in the light of the new situation. The new approach would emphasize "national rejuvenation," involving an overt effort to enlarge and assert China's strength. Xi Jinping, who became the head of the Party in 2012 and President in 2013, has continued and amplified this approach. [34]

In the last decade China has thus gradually shifted to what Western observers have called "sharp" or "hard" power, as distinct from its former primary dependence on "soft power," which denotes persuasion, moral example, and non-coercive diplomacy. "Sharp" or "hard" power involves coercion or the employing material resources to influence the behavior of others. It includes the use of financial incentives, bribes, strategic gifts to individual leaders, infrastructure investments abroad, and channeling funds through multilateral institutions with the goal of influencing their policies, as well as a buildup of military strength and projection of military power.

China still exercises soft power in many settings, but now it's with an eye to enhancing the country's global presence and status. The PRC is taking a much more active role in world climate talks (pledging limits to CO2 emissions and joining the Paris climate agreement of 2015), trade negotiations under the auspices of the World Trade Organization, and activities of the United Nations. Beijing now contributes more generously than before to UN peacekeeping and other operations.[35] China and Russia now cooperate in diplomatic efforts to denuclearize North Korea. In the words of Xi Jinping, the People's Republic is now "moving closer to center stage," as shown by the president's first appearance at the conferences of the World Economic Forum in Davos, Switzerland.

However, what is most distinctive about Chinese foreign policy in the last decade is its growing reliance on "hard" or "sharp" power. The PRC has substantially increased military spending. The emphasis under Xi is on the construction of a blue water navy, which will allow China to project its power globally or, as the President puts it, become a "maritime great power." The new approach also involves asserting claims to new territories that will help with power projection, such as islands in the South China Sea (some of which Beijing actually creates). It has occupied the disputed Paracel Islands since 1974 and is now building facilities on small atolls or reefs there without agreement of Vietnam or the Philippines, states which also claim rights in that oceanic area. But in other areas of greater interest to Russia, such as Syria, the Chinese are wary of being dragged into Russian foreign policy adventures."[36]

Xi's Belt and Road Initiative (BRI) employs economic, rather than military resources, but it is likewise aimed at projecting power, albeit over trade and investment flows, rather than territory.[37] However, the acquisition of key strategic assets and resources is also a major part of the plan. During the 1990s and 2000s under Jiang, China increased its investments mostly to nearby countries that could provide oil and gas for its rapid growth. Now, under Xi, loans from Chinese state banks have risen dramatically, reaching some $180 billion in 2016, up from about $125 billion in 2013.[38] Among the targets are oil-suppliers Kazakhstan and Turkmenistan, but also Angola and Iran. China's "policy banks" have also lent billions to firms close to Putin, many of them owned or managed by those of his cronies under sanctions from the West.[39] More modest financing has also been directed to Ukraine and Belarus, Russia's closest neighbors.

The vast investment projects under the BRI have been directed to improved transportation overland and by sea, as well as advanced communication and port facilities.

Some sixty or more countries have expressed interest. Of the more than 900 envisioned Belt and Road Initiatives, one hears of highways, rail, and pipeline connections and harbors. One road would lead through the Karakoran mountain range from China, through India, and into Pakistan to the

Gwadar port on the Arabian Sea at an estimated cost $46 billion. And the Chinese are supposed to build a railway from Khorgos, the gateway to Central Asia, all the way to the Caspian. A route through Mongolia has also been publicized. In one of the few industrial projects in Central Asia, the Chinese firm Xiamen will build a plant to process tungsten in Kyrgyzstan and send it to China.[40] The Chinese seem to prefer a railway routing through Central Asia, as opposed to the trans-Siberian one.[41] Some of these projects are of likely concern for Russia since they help to establish a long-term Chinese presence in Central Asia.

Besides providing engineering and labor assistance, China will sell some of its surplus steel and cement to help build up less developed countries while also trying to reduce loss-making steel and coal mines, even at the shrinkage of perhaps two million Chinese jobs. All together, it is reported, some $18 trillion may be available in time from the China Development Bank or "Silk Road Fund," though details are not available.

Recipient countries are finding it hard to pay for these investments. Many of them—Pakistan, Mongolia, Laos, Djibouti, the Maldives, and Sri Lanka—already are in "debt distress."[42] Mongolia, which has its main minerals business with the PRC, required a $5.5 billion bailout from the IMF.[43] One could add the fragile economies of Kyrgyzstan and Tajikistan to the list. Apparently rather little risk assessment has been calculated for these projects, such as the World Bank would normally undertake. Indeed, such investments are now being described by unhappy recipients as "debt-trap diplomacy." This could be a Chinese version of coercive diplomacy. When loans are not repaid, China sometimes insists on takeover or other legal action. For example, when Sri Lanka did not pay for a Chinese-financed seaport at Hambamtota, China took majority control of a patch of land surrounding it and reportedly demanded intelligence about sea traffic in the vicinity. Other developing countries have taken note. But with its high yen valuation, growing tourism by Chinese citizens abroad, and protective tariffs on China's cheap steel, the PRC's trade surplus nearly disappeared in 2018 and is predicted to be negative in 2019.[44] That would mean much less cash for such ventures as the BRI.

With the scuttling of the American-led Pacific trade pact by President Trump, China has been invigorating its substitute, the "Regional Comprehensive Economic Partnership," with sixteen regional states, an initiative first announced in 2012. How the smaller countries of South Asia will deal with China's increased power—for example, by engaging Australia, India, or the United States in new ways—will be a possible future development. It does not seem to us that Russia will have either the will or the capability to intervene.

CHINA V. RUSSIA

As we have seen, the history of Sino-Russian relations since 1949 has involved both close cooperation and intense rivalry, once even outright hostility and armed conflict. This mixed legacy is reflected in the complex relationship between the two neighbors that exists today. Although the hostility has been overcome, the relationship remains both cooperative and competitive.

The two countries share some common views of the contemporary international system and the ways in which it should function,[45] as well as some common beliefs about the proper role of the state and the relationship it should have with its own people. They also have some important common interests.[46] Their bilateral trade relationship is highly useful to both, resting as it does on complementary economic structures. Both have a major stake in combatting threats, Islamist and otherwise, from South Asia. They have some distinctive regional concerns which, however, do not bring them into conflict. China is primarily focused on its position in East, and to a lesser extent Southeast Asia. Russia is especially worried about military and political developments on its western border and is eager to reassert its influence in the Middle East. They do not interfere or, at present, even compete with one another in these regions, even if they don't always offer one another diplomatic support for their respective activities.

However, their interests do conflict in some important ways, and this conflict may grow in the future. The price at which Russia sells its resources to China is already a contentious issue. China's involvement in Russia's economy is both helpful and concerning to Moscow. The Russian government is striving to stem the flow of cheap goods from China that compete with its own manufactures. There are worries about the inflow of Chinese migrants. In the future, China's growing global assertivism may clash with Russia's. Already both are seeking to enhance their influence and presence in the Middle East, Africa, the Arctic and even Latin America.

With regard to the Near Abroad, which is President Putin's chief concern, it is fair to remark that China has both helped him achieve his goals and objectives and hindered him from doing so. Putin's actions in Ukraine have been the most dramatic and assertive of all the steps the President has taken to secure Russia's position in the Near Abroad. Nothing else has been so important to him in his quest to keep NATO at bay and prevent democratic regime change. However, Putin's policies there have produced a powerful backlash from the West in the form of economic sanctions, followed by costly counter-sanctions the Russian Federation government has imposed. Russia's economic relationship with China has been critical in helping Putin endure the fall-off in Western trade and investment and compensate his politically essential cronies for the losses they have suffered.

The situation in Central Asia, on the other hand, is very different. Possibly China's massive investments there have contributed to the maintenance of political stability, which Putin also seeks. However, in the last decade China has clearly replaced Russia as the dominant economic force in that region. Putin's hopes to tie the Central Asian economies closely to Russia's have been thwarted by Beijing's policies. Up to now, it is true, China has avoided significant political involvement and has established only a very limited military presence, chiefly along the border between Afghanistan and Tajikistan. But that could change. Chinese maps show ancient positions of the Tang dynasty in Central Asia, where horses were obtained for warfare. Elsewhere in the world, as we have noted in Chapter 1, China's economic initiatives have been followed by an expanding military and political role, probably intended to safeguard its investments and secure its economic position. China has already thwarted some of Putin's key aims in Central Asia. It may do so even more in the future.

At present, we would summarize, the overall relationship between Russia and China is primarily cooperative but contains some competitive elements. It can be plausibly described as a partnership, one which Western policies have helped to fortify. However, the balance between cooperation and competition can shift in the years to come just as it has in the past.

NOTES

1. China grew at rates up to 8 percent per year until 2014 and by less than 7 percent since, with a consumption-led slowdown in 2018-19 to perhaps 6 percent. (This estimate is doubted by knowledgeable economists: C.T. Hsieh and three co-authors, based on the value added tax and other statistics, estimate that China's GDP was overstated by up to 2 percent and investment by seven percent each year from 2008 through 2016, thus overstating the 2016 level by 16 percent. *The Economist,* March 9, 2019.)

2. IMF, *Report for Selected Countries* (April 2019); IMF, *World Economic Outlook Database* (April 2019).

3. *The Economist*, October 20, 2018, citing the Congressional Budget Office, IMF, and SIPRI.

4. Bruno Maçães, *The Dawn of Eurasia* (New Haven, CT:Yale University Press, 2018), 155.

5. "From its very beginning [the Chinese Communist Party] received direct guidance, support, and assistance from the Soviet Union and Comintern" writes a Chinese historian. Nui Jun, *From Yan'an to the World*, trans. Steven I. Levine (Minneapolis, MN: Eastview, 2017), 317. Founded by Moscow in 1919, the Comintern or Communist International served as a means for the Soviets to control the international Communist movement until its dissolution in 1943.

6. Many in the Party resented Soviet efforts to direct the course of revolution in China, believing that Moscow was out of touch with the situation there and was offering inappropriate advice. Tony Saich, *The Chinese Communist Party during the Era of the Comintern (1919-1943)*, n.d. www.sites.hks.harvard.edu/fs/asaich/chinese-communisty-party-during-comintern. pdf

7. Some of the formerly Chinese-held areas were never returned. William Sunderland, *The Baron's Cloak: A History of the Russian Empire in War and Revolution* (Ithaca, New York: Cornell University, 2014).

8. When the Chinese Republic under Sun Yat-Sen ousted the Qing dynasty in 1911, Mongolia declared its independence with the support of Tsarist Russia.

9. During the Soviet period Mongolia was ruled by a Communist regime and was effectively a satellite of the USSR. China, whose forces had lost control of the region in the 1920s, never accepted the legitimacy of its independence. After World War II, the Chinese Communists hoped to regain it. Mao raised the issue when he met with Stalin, but the Soviet leader insisted that the country remain independent. Forty years later, the Chinese still regarded Mongolian independence as unacceptable, complaining (to President G.W. Bush) that Stalin had arbitrarily "severed" the region from China. Sergey Radchenko, "The Truth about Mongolia's Independence 70 Years Ago," *The Diplomat*, October 22, 2015.

10. Prior to China's entry into the war, Stalin promised Mao he would provide the supplies and weaponry he needed for the purpose. Not wanting an armed confrontation with the United States but anxious to preserve Kim Il Sung's control over the northern half of the peninsula, Stalin was relieved when the Chinese did the job for him. Kathryn Weathersby, "Soviet Arms in Korea and the Origins of the Korean War, 1945–1950: New Evidence from the Russian Archives," Working Paper No. 8, Woodrow Wilson Center, November, 1993.

11. Mike Dash, "Khrushchev in Water Wings: On Mao, Humiliation and the Sino-Soviet Split," www.Smithsonian.com May 4, 2012.

12. Chen Jian, "The Tibetan Rebellion of 1959 and China's Changing Relationship with India and the Soviet Union," *Journal of Cold War Studies* 8:3 (Summer, 2006), 90–94. China's efforts to assert control over former imperial territories has remained a point of contention for decades, with the issue flaring up again in 1979, when the PRC fought briefly along its common border with Vietnam, then a Russian ally.

13. Alexander Lukin, *China and Russia* (Cambrdige, UK: Polity, 2018), 174. See Chapter 1 for the larger strategy underlying this vision.

14. *Russia Matters*, September 2018.

15. Indirect exports through Kyrgyzstan would increases this statistic significantly.

16. The S-400 is described in Western sources as "one of the best air-defense systems ever made" and "one of the most sophisticated in the world." Russia's decision to supply it to Turkey, a NATO member, has been much more controversial. "Turkey and Russia cozy up on

missiles," *The Economist*, May 4, 2017; "U.S. gives Turkey ultimatum on Russian missiles," *BBC*, June 9, 2019.

17. "Russia inks contract with China on Su-35 deliveries," TASS, November 19, 2015.

18. Marlene Laruelle and Jean Radvanyi, *Understanding Russia* (Lanham, MD: Rowman & Littlefield, 2018), 74, citing Andrei Borisov.

19. *The Wall Street Journal,* February 1, 2019.

20. 92 percent of Chinese citizens are ethnic Han, the remainder are various Muslim (Hi, Uighur, Kazakh) and other minorities. Muslims constitute somewhat more than 6.5 percent of the population of the Russian Federation; ethnic Russians are approximately 80 percent.

21. President Xi Jinping "declared solemnly in the report of the 19th National Congress that China's development is no threat to other countries and that China will never seek expansion." Zeng Rong, spokesman of the Chinese Embassy in London, *The Economist* , January 6, 2018.

22. Andrew Higgins, "300,000 Troops and 900,000 Tanks: Russia's Biggest Military Drills since Cold War," *The New York Times*, August 28, 2018.

23. Observers have pointed out that because Russia and China do not have a formal military alliance, their joint exercises have not involved complex integrated operations. Their intent appears to be more political than practical: both seem to want to demonstrate their developing security partnership. Franz-Stefan Gady, "Russia to Send Anti-Submarine Warfare Destroyers to South China Sea," *The Diplomat*, August 31, 2016.

24. Alexander Gabuev, "China and Russia's Dangerous Entente," *The Wall Street Journal*, October 4, 2017, printed at https://carnegie.ru/2017/10/04/china-and-russia-s-dangerous-entente-pub-73310

25. *The Wall Street Journal,* February 1, 2019. Quoted in *Russia Matters,* February 1, 2019.

26. James M. Dorsey, *China and the Middle East* (Singapore: Palgrave Macmillan, 2018): 74.

27. Meghan O'Sullivan, *Windfall* (New York: Simon & Shuster, 2017), 226–7.

28. The Amur River alone is 1,780 miles long.

29. Judith Thornton, "Regional Challenges: The Case of Siberia," in Michael Alexeev and Shlomo Weber, *The Oxford Handbook of the Russian Economy* (New York: Oxford, 2013), 687–88.

30. Sources quoted in O'Sullivan, 199 and 413n.

31. Gabuev, "China and Russia's Dangerous Entente."

32. O'Sullivan, 200.

33. *The Economist*, September 15, 2018.

34. Rush Doshi, "Hu's to blame for China's foreign assertiveness?" Brookings, January 22, 2019.

35. In fact, China has become one of the largest contributors to the UN budget. Evan Osnos, "Making China Great Again," *The New Yorker,* January 1, 2018.

36. Bobo Lo, *A Wary Embrace* (Australia: Lowy Institute-Penguin, 2017).

37. Doshi, "Hu's to blame."

38. *The Economist*, December 16, 2017.

39. Alexander Gabuev, "China and Russia's Dangerous Entente."

40. Almaz Kumenov, "Chinese company helps Kazakhstan become tungsten leader," *Eurasianet*, January 18, 2019.

41. Alexander Lukin, Speech in Washington, D.C., *Russia Matters,* October 16, 2018. A Chinese informant of his praised the traffic on the new line from Chengdu to Poland using some Russian lines. .

42. The Centre for Global Development listed twenty-three countries involved in the Bridge and Road Initiative "that were at 'significant' risk of debt distress." Pakistan, the largest

recipient of BRI projects "is facing balance of payments crisis and has begged China for easier terms." *The Economist*, February 2, 2019.

43. Despite considerable real growth since 2010, Mongolia has suffered from price cuts on copper and coal, resulting in a 40 percent depreciation of its *tugrik* currency and considerable unemployment. Both of its governing parties have been accused of corruption.

44. *The Economist*, March 16, 2019.

45. Alexander Lukin, *China and Russia*, 193.

46. Dmitri Trenin, *China Daily*, September 11, 2018, quoted in *Russia Matters*, accessed October 1, 2018.

Chapter Eight

Conclusions and Prospects

Our study of some sixteen neighbors[1] of the Russian Federation has inquired whether and to what degree Russian policies toward those neighbors under President Vladimir Putin have helped to secure Russia's dominance of what it calls the "Near Abroad," thereby contributing to the restoration of Russia's great power status. Attaining that status has been the central focus of his foreign policy. Have the collective arrangements initiated by Moscow and its bilateral relations with the states in the Near Abroad contributed to Putin's main policy objectives there? How has Russia's cooperation with China affected Moscow's position in the Near Abroad and beyond? Based on the President's statements and actions, we believe he has sought to achieve four key objectives in the Near Abroad:

1. preventing radical democratic political changes which might undermine his autocratic regime in the Russian Federation
2. excluding NATO from countries near Russia's borders
3. interdicting flows of terrorists, arms, and drugs (or drug-related communicable diseases)
4. providing generous incomes for Putin's closest associates and supporters.

We have shown that Putin's nearly two-decade rule has had considerable, although not unqualified, success in achieving these objectives in the Near Abroad, contributing to his larger aim of restoring Russia as a great power in

133

world politics. Let us review what we have shown in Chapters 2–7 concerning these four key objectives.

(1) At home President Putin has kept his highly centralized government in power within the Russian Federation through five electoral victories by big margins.[2] As of October 2018, he maintained a 66 percent approval rating, according to a survey by the highly respected Levada Center.[3] Why? As long as oil and gas revenues were flowing, most Russians enjoyed higher real incomes and, for some, access to foreign travel. Most Russians we have spoken to approve of Putin's assertive foreign policies in the Near Abroad because, as we heard on several occasions, Russians take pride in the restoration of their country's big power status.[4] Most of them reject criticisms of those policies from the United States and Europe. The broad public seems to believe the controlled Russian press and television, which echo the official line of the Kremlin. The media almost uniformly insist, for example, that the Crimean takeover was defensive and both the Ukrainian Orange Revolution in 2004 and the Euromaidan demonstrations in 2014 had fascist ambitions. Throughout most of the Near Abroad, where Western newspapers are hard to find, Russian media maintain the Kremlin position. The BBC, Voice of America and Radio Liberty are not influential, if they are heard at all.

Putin's response to the challenge of democratic revolution in Ukraine in 2004 included a series of measures to enhance his government's power at home, and these have been notably successful. The Russian President directly controls public activity in Russia by appointing many government and enterprise officials throughout the Federation's extended territory. Putin's own political party, United Russia, dominates the State Duma (parliament) and has no realistic rival.[5] Well-known opposition politicians have been mysteriously slain, imprisoned, or prevented from running for office. Homegrown demonstrations of liberally minded citizens have occurred in Moscow and other Russian cities but have met police repression or were dissipated. At the same time, continued free emigration of disaffected intellectuals and youth, as well as ambitious entrepreneurs, has provided a safety valve. Although some initiatives from below have been allowed more recently, nothing that Putin forbids can succeed within Russia.

It is true that anti-Russian "color" regimes have taken power for a time in Kyrgyzstan, Georgia, and Ukraine, as we have detailed in Chapters 4 and 5. However, various measures, especially military occupation in Georgia and Ukraine, have helped to prevent these events from triggering mass protests in Russia that might have threatened Putin's rule. The brief and unthreatening

"Tulip Revolution" in tiny Kyrgyzstan lasted only until Moscow withdrew critical material support from its democratically elected presidents. The financial support of smaller post-Soviet southern republics (Armenia, Kyrgyzstan, and Tajikistan) and breakaway territories (Abkhazia, South Ossetia, and Transdnistria) has been given to support friendly, mostly autocratic regimes, even if Russia's economic weakness and its own domestic and security needs now prevent it from doing more. In Armenia, where Russians own vital structures, democratically elected governments have kept to an inoffensive stance. The West has challenged Russia's self-proclaimed right to "pre-emptive use of military force in the CIS countries,"[6] but that has not deterred Moscow from sustaining its deployments in or near defiant states in the Near Abroad.

China assists Putin's efforts to sustain his own and his government's power by lending international support for (or at least refraining from criticizing) his attempts to counter democratic change in the Near Abroad. The People's Republic also helps to legitimize Putin's autocratic style of rule by challenging Western models of democratic theory and practice as embodied in NATO and the European Union (see Chapter 7).

(2) Russia was unable to prevent NATO accession of the three Baltic countries in 2004 but has been able to keep Ukraine or Georgia from joining the organization, as both have indicated a desire to do. Russian occupation of western Ukraine by irregular troops may well have been motivated by this objective. Russia has recognized parts of Georgia as independent states. NATO is reluctant to take on either of these countries as members until their boundaries are settled and decisive political arrangements made with Russia. Military exercises in Belarus are intended to deter any NATO threat, and Russia has made it clear that further enlargement would constitute an unacceptable provocation.

Nevertheless, Putin's increased defense spending, military modernization and, more recently, new forward deployments, have stimulated potentially defensive measures by the members of NATO in the areas close to Russia. This in itself recognizes Russia's great power, without posing a significant military challenge. Though remaining neutral, Finland cooperates with NATO defense arrangements in the Baltic Sea area along with NATO members, Estonia, Latvia, Lithuania, and Poland. To these actions Russia has responded with cyber-warfare and fake broadcasts, as well as an increased military presence, all of which contribute to its deterrent capabilities. Russia's efforts to limit the growth of NATO power on its borders are thus largely, although not entirely, successful (see Chapter 6).

(3) Communicable diseases and drug addiction may have their roots in substances entering through the Near Abroad but are spread within Russia by social contacts among Russians themselves. These have not been effectively countered by Russia inadequate health services, which have been cut by Putin in favor of more military spending.

Russia has been more successful in preventing radical Islamic groups from entering the Federation by placing border troops in Tajikistan and consulting with the governments of Uzbekistan and Turkmenistan about threats from Taliban and ISIS. All the states of Central Asia have been helpful in protecting Russia's southern borders. Although difficult to estimate, Russia has probably been spared some influx of terrorists, who have been stopped by the Uzbek authorities, among others. On Putin's watch, there have been troubling periods of civil turbulence in Tajikistan, Kyrgyzstan, and Uzbekistan. They have been effectively suppressed with Russia's encouragement and assistance. In the future a new authoritarian leader, perhaps Islamist, could arise, denounce Russian "imperialism" and appeal to another power (such as Saudi Arabia, Pakistan, or a Taliban-dominated Afghanistan) for arms and support. Such a leader might have a natural audience in Central Asia, where every state has a Muslim majority. Such a development could have destabilizing consequences in Russia, which contains 15–20 million citizens of the Muslim faith. However, Islamism has thus far held limited attraction for moderate and mostly quite secular Central Asian Muslims. The Taliban have limited their advances to Afghanistan and Pakistan. Despite external aid to Muslim rebels in Chechnya, some of it passing through the Near Abroad, maintenance of a strict regime in Chechnya under the control of a loyal protégé, along with other domestic security measures, has likewise limited the impact of Muslim opposition within the Russian Federation. China's efforts have ensured that increased migration into Siberia has not presented an ideological or political threat. In other words, even if his policies in the Near Abroad have not completely succeeded in keeping out undesirable people, objects and influences, they have been sufficient to meet the challenges Putin faces (see Chapter 4).

(4) Russia's elite draw financial benefits from four sources, according to an important study by liberal Russian politicians Boris Nemtsov and Vladimir Milov: privileged public procurement, stock manipulation, asset stripping, and privileged trade. Special Gazprom rake-offs from Russia's continued export of oil and gas alone during 2004–2007 amounted to $60 billion.[7] The country has seventy-four billionaires, according to Credit Suisse. This is

a surprisingly large number for a country of Russia's recent Communist past.[8] Proceeds appear to be sufficient to enrich those oligarchs remaining in the country, to build expensive projects such as those required by the Olympics and World Cup, or to renovate parts of Moscow, and to build some exorbitantly expensive roads. One of the most costly consequences of the annexation of Crimea was a nineteen-kilometer bridge (Europe's longest) connecting it to Russia over the Kerch Strait. This span avoids the land link through Ukraine, which is often a site of considerable violence. It was constructed by a company owned by Arkady Rotenberg, an associate of Putin's, at a cost of $4 billion.[9] Crimea has required new electricity connections, too, and establishing these has also led to profits for Putin's domestic allies.

True, much of the oil and gas once sent northward from Central Asia and then sold profitably to the West is now flowing through pipelines to China and Europe via non-Russian territory, resulting in the loss of a significant part of the revenues that once went to the state- and crony-run Gazprom and Rosneft operations (see Chapter 4). Staples such as cotton, uranium, gold, and rare-earth minerals are now easily transported and sold in world markets by the Central Asian states themselves, so the former rake-off by Russian enterprise managers is no longer available. However, the EaEU promises some gains to Russian firms from its protective tariffs against Chinese and other consumer goods produced abroad (see Chapter 3).[10]

Taking these four key objectives into account, we would judge Putin's policies toward his neighbors to have been a reasonable, if not unqualified, success from his point of view. Russia's dominance of its Near Abroad has been furthered by many of the steps he has taken, even if China has made considerable inroads into that dominance in the economic sphere. Thus Putin's policies toward his neighbors have aided him in his quest to restore Russia's great power status. Those policies have been tailored well to the different situations in the three regions of the Near Abroad we have identified in Chapters 4–6: minimally necessary support for the five weak or authoritarian rulers to the south; military assistance, occupation or threats for the five in the southwest, and deterrence against NATO and expansion of its presence on Russia's borders in the northwest. Diplomatic, economic and military cooperation with China has been positive so far, despite the benefits the People's Republic has obtained at Russia's expense in Central Asia.

Therefore, we cannot agree with the position taken by the well-known expert Marlene Laruelle and her co-author, Jean Radvanyi, in a new, very well documented book, *Understanding Russia*. She writes, "This difficulty [the inequality among interdependent states] in organizing the post-Soviet space in a constructive fashion is *one of the major failures of Russian foreign policy.*"[11] To be sure, the multilateral organizations which Russia has organized (Chapter 3) have contributed little, but they hardly constitute a "failed strategy." Appropriate bilateral deals and military placements in all three regions (Chapters 4–6) have helped achieve Putin's objectives. As they also write, in connection with the Syrian intervention, "Russia is again a major actor on the international scene." [12] In our view, without the stable (if hardly ideal) neighborhood achieved by Putin over the last nineteen years, those out-of-neighborhood ventures would not have been possible.

PROSPECTS FOR THE FUTURE

Meeting these four objectives in the Near Abroad and thus helping to restore Russia's great power status do not guarantee a prosperous Russian future. That is because Putin has failed to diversify the Russian economy away from its heavy dependence on export of oil and gas, for which demand is likely to decline in the future (see Chapter 2). Though once a scientific and technological global leader, Russia has been suffering from the fact that many of the most talented young people and successful entrepreneurs have been leaving the country. Some are attracted by better medical care and educational opportunities for their children, sectors the regime has neglected in favor of higher military spending for the last decade. Russia's repressive political atmosphere and weak legality are also dismaying to many intellectuals and members of the business community. This resembles the departure of brilliant and ambitious young people from Germany after the Nazi takeover and from China even today. In all likelihood, few of these emigres will ever return permanently, but Russia's (and China's) competitors in the West will undoubtedly benefit, as they have already.

One remedy for Russia's economic weakness would be substantial foreign investment. Putin has shown considerable interest in such a prospect. However, as we have seen, he appears to be ambivalent about China as a source of such funds. This may be partly owing to the fact that it is Russia's energy resources that have been Beijing's major focus. Another possible source of external funds is Japan, which is similarly hungry for Russian energy but is also interested in a wide variety of other ventures. However, Putin's ability to attract Japanese investment has been severely constrained by his unwillingness up to now to placate Japan by yielding control over the southern Kurile Islands. These were taken by Soviet forces in 1945 but are claimed by Japan.[13] The victorious United States returned the Ryuku and other islands to Japan's sovereignty long ago, but Russia refuses to accede to Japan's strong interest in this tiny real estate, despite an agreement in 1956 to re-establish diplomatic relations along with the return of the two smaller of the four islands in dispute. This agreement has never been fulfilled.[14] Were the Russians to resolve the issue, they would gain Japanese funds for developing Siberia, the Far East and the Arctic, balancing China's position and benefitting the Russian economy enormously. Numerous top level discussions with Japan's leaders have not surmounted this hurdle. Even without such a concession and a peace treaty based on it, Japan has been willing to invest in projects in Sakhalin and the Transneft Pipeline.[15] The Japanese Ambassador to Russia has indicated interest in Russian pharmaceutical plants, and discussions have featured a plan to extend the Trans-Siberian Railroad to Hokkaido via bridges, as a route from Japan to Europe. In 2016, following the imposition of Western sanctions, Russia also welcomed the possibility of major energy ventures.

These overtures are likely to be followed up, however, only if Putin is willing and able to concede to Japan's demand regarding the Kurils. As of now, that does not seem to be in the cards. Russia has been steadily increasing its military presence on the islands on Putin's watch.[16] The Russian President has voiced his concern that if the islands were to be returned to Japanese control, American troops might be deployed there.[17] In addition to these strategic considerations, Putin must contend with growing public opposition to returning the islands. Russian nationalists are adamant in opposing such a move: that would mean surrendering part of the territory Russia gained in its hard-won victory in World War II. This is something they could never countenance, especially in the wake of Russia's loss of the Baltic States. They have become much more active and vocal since the annexation of Crimea in 2014, which appears to have unleashed a groundswell of intense nationalist passion. At the same time, there seems to be much public sympathy for the nationalists' views. Whatever Putin's personal preferences may be, it will be hard for him to ignore these pressures. Precisely because his government has entered a period of resource constraint in which Japanese assistance is particularly desirable, the Russian leader is encountering a great deal of public discontent from cutbacks he has had to make in social spending and cannot afford to alienate the nationalists, who have provided much needed political support.[18]

Returning Crimea to Ukraine and agreeing to a peaceful settlement in Donets and Luhansk provinces would probably result in termination of European and American sanctions. Significant Western investment in Russia might well follow. Russia would thereby gain access to advanced Western technology that would help substantially with the modernization the Russian economy so badly needs. [19]

Since we believe Putin will not agree to reverse his foreign policy gains or be able to diversify the economy, which is now committed to state-run enterprises, including big banks and energy giants run by trusted personalities, the likelihood of economic recovery to match the challenge of China is slight. With prospects dim for foreign investments or growth of the labor force, stagnation is likely to be the result. The IMF projects a growth of 1.5 percent to 2021. The government will come under increasing pressure to allocate funds to pensions and neglected health and education systems. New (fifth generation) military technology required for superpower status will be desirable, but it may be unaffordable. Annexation of Ukraine's eastern provinces, however much the President might like to accomplish it, will be beyond his means, as will any significant spending to retain the loyalty of Russia's allies in the Near Abroad. Putin's quest for great power status, both in the Near Abroad and beyond, thus may be severely constrained by Russia's economic weakness.

NOTES

1. Not all the "neighbors" we consider have a common border with Russia, but those that do not were historically part of the Soviet Union and the Russian Empire before it and thus are part of the "Near Abroad," in which Russia claims a "privileged interest." Putin's ambitions in this sphere and his ability to fulfill them are our central focus (see Chapter 1). We say little about Norway and Poland, which do have short borders with Russia. However, they are incorporated in our discussion of Russia's northwestern border in Chapter 6. Mongolia and North Korea, which also share a border with Russia, are likewise dealt with, but only briefly. They figure into our discussion of Russia's relationship with China in Chapter 7. Japan has a tiny, disputed border with the Russian Federation among the Kuril Islands north of Hokkaido, while the U.S. state of Alaska (once part of the Russian Empire) shares access to the Bering Sea along with Siberia. Both inevitably make an appearance, but are not a focus of discussion in this volume. Detailed consideration of Russia's relations with Japan and the United States would require a different book, one whose focus was not primarily on the Near Abroad.

2. As we note in Chapter 1, to comply with the provisions of the Russian Constitution in effect at the time, Putin installed his protégé, Dmitri Medvedev, as President in 2008, retaining for himself the position of Prime Minister. However, Medvedev's electoral success is uniformly attributed to Putin's backing for him and may therefore be considered one of Putin's victories.

3. Putin's approval rating reached an all-time high of 87 percent in August, 2014, soon after his wildly popular annexation of Crimea. In other words, this extraordinary rating was a direct result of his policies in the Near Abroad. Analysts attribute his relatively low, if still enviable, rating of 66 percent in October, 2018, to the fact that he had recently signed into law a provision to raise the retirement age in Russia. "Putin's Approval Rating the Lowest Since 2013—Poll," *The Moscow Times*, October 25, 2018.

4. "They may consider Russia greatness on the international stage to be Putin's main accomplishment, but the public is growing disillusioned with Russia's isolation, the unresolved conflict with the West, and the fact that the country is constantly 'helping others' at the expense of its own citizens." Denis Volkov, Levada Centre, *The Economist,* December 1, 2018. More than half of Russian respondents hold Putin responsible for the country's problems. "Majority of Russians Hold Putin Responsible for Rising Costs of Living, Poll Says," *Moscow Times,* December 13, 2018.

5. As of 2018, United Russia controlled almost 75 percent of the seats in the Duma.

6. *Nezavisimaya Gaz*eta, October 24, 2003, quoted in Robert H. Donaldson, Joseph L Nogee, and Vidya Nadkarni. *The Foreign Policy of Russia, Changing Systems, Enduring Interests,* 5th ed. (Armonk, New York: M.E. Sharpe, 2014), 210, 229 n. 128. Of course Russia also uses "adaptive tactics," quite different from the use of force.

7. Boris Nemstov and Vladimir Milov, "Putin i Gazprom," *Novaya Gazeta,* cited in Anders Åslund, *Russia's Crony Capitalism (*New Haven, CT: Yale University Press, 2019): 154. Nemtsov was murdered under suspicious circumstances in 2015, following his audacious criticism of Putin's policies in Ukraine.

8. *Russia Matters,* accessed October 29, 2018. Credit Suisse reports that the top ten percent of Russians own 82 percent of its household wealth, a greater concentration than in the United States and one of the highest in the world.

9. Anton Troianovski, "Putin's bridge to Crimea illustrates his power—and his regime's weak spot," *Washington Post*, May 15, 2018.

10. Because such gains are so important for Putin, who must purchase the loyalty of the CEO's of at least some of Russian's largest firms, planned talks with China on a free trade agreement with the EaEU are unlikely to produce results. Igor Shuvalov, First Deputy Prime Minister, held out the possibility of such an agreement at a meeting of the Supreme Eurasian Economic Council in Astana, Kazakhstan in 2016. He said that "non-tariff barriers in bilateral trade" would fall first. *Vesti,* May 31, 2016. We are grateful to A. Lukin, *China and Russia* (Cambridge, UK: Polity, 2018), 170, for this reference. Apparently, "free trade" refers to certain specified goods only, not yet identified.

11. Marlene Laruelle and Jean Radvanyi, *Understanding Russia* (Lanham, MD: Rowman & Littlefield, 2018), 111. (Our emphasis.)

12. Laruelle and Radvanyi, 93.

13. "Southern Kurils" is the term Russia uses; Japan refers to them as its "Northern Territories."

14. Artyom Lukin, "Russia and Japan: A Deal Is Still Possible," *Asia Pacific Policy Society Policy Forum*, February 4, 2019; *The Economist*, February 9, 2019.

15. "Russia-Japan Investment Fund nakes first investments of $170 mln," Reuters, December 6, 2017. Prime Minister Abe has promised investments in the Russian Far East and proposed "shared sovereignty" in the Kurils; Lukin, "Russia and China."

16. Russia constructed several anti-ship missile complexes there in 2016; in 2017 Russia's Defense Minister announced that his country would deploy three divisions on the islands in order to protect them, and plans to build a Russian naval base on the Kurils were made public soon after. Aleksandra Bausheva, "Russia and Japan on Different Wavelengths in the Kuril

Islands," Center for Strategic and International Studies, *New Perspectives on Foreign Policy* 15 (Spring, 2018).

17. Bausheva, "Russia and Japan."

18. Andrew Higgins, "Putin Quashes Japanese Hopes of End to Island Dispute," *New York Times*, January 22, 2019.

19. Japanese investment might also flow more readily. America's secondary sanctions on foreign investors in Russia's economy are increasingly an obstacle. Maria Shagina, "Japan and Russia: star-crossed economic partners?" *Asia Pacific Policy Society Policy Forum*, April 2, 2019.

Bibliography

Alexseev, Michael, and Shlomo Weber. *The Oxford Handbook of the Russian Economy*. New York: Oxford, 2013.

Argumenti i Fakti (Moscow).

Asian Security.

Åslund, Anders. *Russia's Crony Capitalism: The Path from Market Economy to Kleptocracy*. New Haven, CT: Yale University Press, 2019.

Baker Institute for Public Policy Issue Briefs.

Belarus News (Minsk).

BBC News and World Service.

www.Bloomberg.com.

Brookings Institution Reports.

www.Carnegie.ru. (Carnegie Center Moscow)

Center on Global Interests Reports.

Central Asian Survey.

Central Asia-Caucasus Analyst.

www.cfr.org. (Council on Foreign Relations)

Chatham House Reports.

China Daily.

CIA Factbook (2018).

Comparative Economic Studies.

Council on Foreign Relations Reports.

Cooley, Alexander, and John Heatherstraw. *Dictators Without Borders*. New Haven, CT: Yale University Press, 2017.

Cornell, Svante E., and S. Frederick Starr. *The Guns of August 2008: Russia's War in Georgia*. Armonk, NY: M.E. Sharpe, 2009.

Crisis Group Asia (International).

The Current Digest of the Russian Press. East View Press, weekly. Abbreviated in endnotes as CD, followed by the volume, number, and pages.

Dawisha, Karen. *Putin's Kleptocracy*. New York: Simon & Shuster, 2014.

Donaldson, Robert H., Joseph L Nogee, and Vidya Nadkarni. *The Foreign Policy of Russia, Changing Systems, Enduring Interests*, 5th ed. Armonk, NY: M.E. Sharpe, 2014.

Dorsey, James M. *China and the MiddleEast*. Singapore: Palgrave Macmillan, 2018.

East Asia Forum.

www.ec.europa.eu. *(European Commission).*

Eurasia Daily Monitor.

Eurasianet.

Eurasia Review.

Euronews. (Newsletter of the UK Network of Euro Info Centres).

European Council on Foreign Relations Reports.

Europe-Asia Studies.

Financial Express.

Financial Times.

Forbes.

Foreign Affairs.

Foreign Policy.

Gates, Robert. *Memoirs of a Secretary at War.* London: Allen, 2014.

Gazette of Central Asia.

Globe and Mail.

Georgetown Journal of International Affairs.

Grigas, Agnia. *Beyond Crimea. The New Russian Empire.* New Haven, CT: Yale University Press, 2016.

Harvard International Review.

Interfax.

Interfax Kazakhstan.

International Monetary Fund (IMF) Reports.

Izvestia.

Journal of Cold War Studies.

Journal of International Affairs.

Journal of International Security Affairs.

Johnson's Russia List.

Jun, Nui. *From Yan'an to the World.* Translated by Steven I. Levine. Minneapolis, MN: Eastview, 2017.

Kanet, Roger, and Matthew Sussex. *Foreign Policy in a Contested Region.* New York: Palgrave-Macmillan, 2015.

Kivelson, Valerie A., and Ronald Grigor Suny. *Russia's Empires.* New York: Oxford University Press, 2017.

Kommersant (Moscow).

Laruelle, Marlene, ed. *The Central Asia-Afghanistan Relationship.* Lanham, MD: Lexington, 2017.

Laruelle, Marlene, and Sebastian Peyrouse. *Globalizing Central Asia.* Armonk, NY: M.E. Sharpe, 2013.

Laruelle, Marlene, and Jean Radvanyi. *Understanding Russia: The Challenges of Transformation.* Lanham, MD: Rowman & Littlefield, 2018.

Libman, Aleksander, and Evgeny Vinokurov. *Holding Together Regionalism: Twenty Years of Post-Soviet Integration.* London: Palgrave-Macmillan, 2012.

Lo, Bobo. *A Wary Embrace.* Australia: Penguin Random House, 2017.

Lukin, Alexander. *China and Russia: The New Rapprochement.* Cambridge, UK: Polity, 2018.

Maçães, Bruno. *The Dawn of Eurasia.* New Haven, CT: Yale University Press, 2018.

Marat, Erica. *The Military and the State in Central Asia.* London: Routledge, 2010.

Menon, Rajan, and Eugene Rumer. *Conflict in Ukraine.* Cambridge, MA: MIT, 2015.

Miller, Chris. *Putinomics: Power and Money in Resurgent Russia.* Chapel Hill, NC: University of North Carolina Press, 2018.

Misiunas, Romuald J., and Rein Taagepera, *The Baltic States: Years of Dependence, 1940-1990.* Berkeley: University of California Press, 1993.

Modern Diplomacy.

NBC News.

Newsweek.

New Eastern Europe.

New Times (Moscow).

Nezavisimaia Gazeta (Moscow).

Novaia Gazeta (Moscow).

NPR (National Public Radio).

Nu, Jun. *From Ya'nan to the World.* Moscow: Eastview, 2017.

Ohanyan, Anna, ed. *Russia Abroad: Driving Regional Fracture in Post-Communist Eurasia and Beyond.* Washington, DC: Georgetown University Press, 2018.

Oliker, Olga, Keith Crane, Lowell H. Schwartz, and Catherine Yusupov. *Russian Foreign Policy: Sources and Implications.* Santa Monica, CA: RAND, 2009.

O'Sullivan, Meghan L. *Windfall: How the New Energy Abundance Upends Global Politics and Strengthens American Power.* New York: Simon & Schuster, 2017.

Pomfret, Richard. *The Central Asian Economies Since Independence.* Princeton, NJ: Princeton University Press, 2006.

Post-Soviet Affairs.

Problems of Post-Communism.

PRI (Public Radio International).

Reuters.

RFE/RL (Radio Free Europe/Radio Liberty).

Russia in Global Affairs (Moscow).

Russia Matters (Belfer Center for Science and International Affairs, Harvard Kennedy School).

Russian Journal of Economics.

Salzman, Rachel S. *Russia, BRICS, and the Disruption of Global Order.* Washington, DC: Georgetown University Press, 2019.

Sanderland, William. *The Baron's Cloak.* Ithaca, NY: Cornell University Press, 2014.

Sengupta, Anita. *Heartlands of Eurasia: The Geopolitics of Political Space.* Lanham, MD: Lexington, 2009.

SIPRI (Stockholm International Peace Research Institute).

Slavic Review.

Spechler, Martin. *The Political Economy of Reform in Central Asia: Uzbekistan under Authoritarianism.* London: Routledge, 2008.

Spechler, Dina R., and Martin C. Spechler. "Uzbekistan among the Great Powers." *Communist and Post-Communist Studies* 42, no.3 (June, 2009), 353–73.

Spechler, Dina R., and Martin C. Spechler. "The International Political Economy of Central Asian Statehood," in Emilian Kavalski, ed. *Stable Outside/Fragile Inside?* Burlington, VT: Ashgate, 2010.

Spechler, Dina R., and Martin C. Spechler. "The Foreign Policy of Uzbekistan." *Central Asian Survey* 29, no. 2 (2010), 159-70.

Spechler, Martin C., Joachim Ahrens, and Herman W. Hoen, *State Capitalism in Eurasia.* Singapore, London, and New Jersey: World Scientific, 2017.

Sputnik (Moscow).

Starr, S. Frederick, and Svante Cornell, eds., *Putin's Grand Strategy: The Eurasian Union and its Discontents.* Washington, DC: Central Asia-Caucasus Institute and Silk Road Studies Program, 2014.

Stent, Angela. *The Limits of Partnership: US-Russian Relations in the Twenty-first Century.* Princeton, NJ: Princeton University Press, 2014.

Stent, Angela. *Putin's World.* New York: Twelve, 2019.

Stratfor.

Sunderland, William. *The Baron's Cloak: A History of the Russian Empire in War and Revolution.* Ithaca, New York: Cornell University, 2014.

TASS (Moscow).

The Diplomat.

The Economist.

The Guardian.

The Moscow Times (Moscow).

The New Republic.

The New York Times.

The New Yorker.

The Times.

The Wall Street Journal.

Tellis, Ashley, Alison Szalinski, and Michael Wills. *Strategic Asia 2019.* Washington, DC: National Bureau of Asian Research, 2019.

Tsygankov, Andrei P. *Russia's Foreign Policy,* fifth ed., Lanham, MD: Rowman & Littlefield, 2019.

USA Today.

Vedomosti (Moscow).

Vinokurov, Evgeny. *Introduction to the Eurasian Economic Union.* (London: Palgrave Macmillan, 2018.

Voice of America (VOA).

Wishnick, Elizabeth. *Mending Fences: The Evolution of Moscow's China Policy from Brezhnev to Yeltsin.* Seattle, WA: University of Washington Press, 2014.

Washington Post.

World Almanac 2018 and 2019. New York: Infobase, 2018, 2019.

World Development Indicators 2014, 2015, 2016. Washington, DC: IBRD, the World Bank, 2014, 2015, and 2016.

Zając, Justyna. *Poland's Security Policy: The West, Russia and the Changing International Order.* London: Palgrave Macmillan, 2016.

Zhukov, Stanislav, and Olga Reznikova. *Tsentral'naia Azia i Kitai: ekonomicheskoe vzaimodeistvie v usloviakh globalizatsia* [Central Asia and China: economic interaction in the context of globalization]. Moscow: IMEMO RAN, 2009.

Index

About the Authors

Dina R. Spechler is Associate Professor of Political Science and Adjunct Associate Professor of International Studies in the Hamilton Lugar School of Global and International Studies, Indiana University. She is a faculty affiliate of the Russian and East European Institute and the Center for the Study of the Middle East, Indiana University. She is a graduate of Radcliffe College and Harvard University (PhD, Government). She teaches Russian foreign policy, comparative foreign policy and international relations. She has published articles, monographs and books on Soviet and Russian foreign policy and domestic politics, including *Domestic Influences on Soviet Foreign Policy; Permitted Dissent in the USSR;* and *Russian Nationalism and Political Stability in the USSR.* With her graduate students, she has researched and written about collective action and economic development in mountain villages in Tajikistan and has conducted interviews for her research in Tajikistan, Uzbekistan, Russia, Ukraine, and Estonia.

Martin C. Spechler is Professor of Economics Emeritus and faculty affiliate of the Russian and East European Institute, Indiana University. He is a graduate of Harvard College and Harvard University (PhD, Economics). During the 1970s and 1980s he served as an economic expert for NATO. Since 1997 Spechler has worked in Central Asia as a consultant for the World Bank, Global Development Network, USAID, and Asian Development Bank's CAREC project, which promotes freer trade and finances roads, infrastructure, and water projects in Central Asia. He was among the first group of

American experts sent by the State Department to lecture and meet with Russian officials.

Martin Spechler is the author of three books and over one hundred articles and book reviews. His new book, *State Capitalism in Eurasia,* authored with a team of Dutch, German, and Russian specialists, was published in 2017 by World Publishing. Sponsored by Volkswagen Foundation, and based on more than two hundred interviews, this volume analyzed the emerging economic systems of Kazakhstan, Uzbekistan, Kyrgyzstan, and the Russian Federation.